FENTRESS BRADBURN ARCHITECTS'
GATEWAY TO THE WEST:

Designing the Passenger Terminal Complex at Denver International Airport

FENTRESS BRADBURN ARCHITECTS'
GATEWAY TO THE WEST:
Designing the Passenger Terminal Complex at Denver International Airport

First published in Australia in 2000 by
The Images Publishing Group Pty Ltd
ACN 059 734 431
6 Bastow Place, Mulgrave, Victoria, 3170
Telephone (61 3) 9561 5544 Facsimile (61 3) 9561 4860

National Library of Australia Cataloguing-in-Publication Data

Bibliography.
Includes index.
ISBN 1 86470 070 X

1. Fentress Bradburn (Firm). 2. Denver International Airport.
3. Airports – Colorado – Denver – Design and construction.
I. Fentress Bradburn (Firm). II. Title. III. Title: Gateway to the west.
(Series: Building monographs).

725.390978883

Author: Jessica Sommers
Copy by Valerie Moses
Edited by Julian Dahl
Designed by The Graphic Image Studio Pty Ltd,
Mulgrave, Australia
Printed in Hong Kong

C O N T E N T S

F O R E W O R D

Airports: Economic Engines and Works of Art
by Federico Peña

1

Imagining, designing and building a new airport for the 21st century is a challenge. Only communities with vision, fortitude and determination can successfully undertake a project of such magnitude. The spectacular and modern Denver International Airport has a global presence that communities around the world are trying to replicate. In the United States, it may be the last new airport built on a green-field site for decades to come.

Millions of citizens fly today. In the United States, the Federal Aviation Administration (FAA) estimates that 900 million people will be flying annually by 2007. Flying domestically has become an essential and sometimes daily form of transportation for many people. International air travel will soon be as affordable and convenient for global travelers.

In the rush to catch a flight or make a connection, most people do not realize that airports are massive economic engines that often serve as the economic backbone of a city, state or region. The effort to build Denver International Airport consumed the energies of thousands of citizens and required years of their passionate hard work. Colorado's economy is experiencing one of the lowest unemployment rates in the nation as a testament to their vision and dedication.

Cities that want to participate in the global economy of the 21st century must have international airports. Those that do not will fall behind. Internet, satellite and fiber optic forms of communication are bringing people closer together as a global community. The more we communicate, the more we will want to experience friendships, communities and places in person. More interaction leads to more travel. More travel brings commerce, tourism and capital. A historical review of any great city today will trace its current successes to a transportation asset: a major seaport, rail connection or airport. In the 21st century, airports will play the predominant role in the growth of communities.

Denver and Colorado are no different. If not for a special rail connection that business leaders brought to Denver decades ago, Cheyenne could have emerged as the center of the region, and without the old Stapleton Airport, Colorado's ski resorts would not have blossomed to become the finest in the world. Thousands of jobs resulted both directly and indirectly from the many years of Stapleton's operations, which helped make Denver a major hub in the national aviation system.

Over time, new safety requirements and growth pressures caused the Denver community to realize that expanding Stapleton Airport was not the solution for the next century. Only a new airport could accommodate all the future needs of our State and region, and address the growing noise issues that were infuriating nearby residents.

From the perspective of economic development, airports are magnets for business expansion. Any airport director will tell you that companies want to build their facilities near airports, or in many cases, on the airport property itself. Now that we shop on the Internet, companies need to get products delivered on time to their customers' doorsteps, and being near an airport provides that competitive edge. High technology companies have moved to Colorado because of our high quality of life and solid work force, but having a close, efficient international airport has also helped win them over.

The new Denver International Airport has five runways. Upon opening, it was the first major airport in the world that could accommodate simultaneous landings on three runways, even in a snowstorm. At Stapleton Airport, only one runway was permitted to operate during similar conditions, causing major delays and cancellations, which often resulted in passengers spending the night at the terminal. Stapleton's inability to operate fully under challenging conditions constituted a "clog" in the national aviation system, which produced further delays and cancellations at airports from New York to California to Texas. Delays like these caused people to avoid Stapleton. One airline even ran national advertisements encouraging flyers to use Salt Lake City as a hub. Nationwide flight delays were worsening, not only causing major inconvenience to millions of passengers, but also having a negative impact on the region's economic productivity in that business people and product shipments were delayed. Stapleton was ranked by the FAA as one of the nation's airports with the worst delays.

As Secretary of Transportation for the Clinton administration in the early and mid-1990s, I saw more broadly the need for a new Denver airport. In reality, it was not a Denver airport: it was a national resource that needed federal attention. At the time, Denver was the fifth busiest airport in the country and one of the nation's key "hubs" in the "hub and spoke" system. If the congestion and delays in Denver could be eliminated, this would reduce delays across the United States and make the national transportation system quantifiably more efficient. The FAA committed $500 million toward the development of Denver International Airport to ensure that the long-standing, significant delays at Stapleton would be eliminated from the national airport system. Unfortunately, similar delays at other major airports in the United States now need to be addressed as millions more people now choose to fly.

Globally we are witnessing a movement to construct more efficient and technologically advanced airports. Hong Kong, Japan, Korea, Mexico and other international centers of trade and commerce understand that these airports are essential to their economies' global competitiveness.

I am proud of the role I played as Mayor of Denver, but even more proud of the thousands of citizens who looked into the future and saw the need for Denver International Airport. They did more. They built not only one of the most efficient and technologically advanced airports in the world, but also one of the most beautiful. Serving as an economic engine for Colorado today and in the future, this airport is a testament to the potential of the human spirit in creating a global gateway recognized throughout the world.

1   Federico Peña

INTRODUCTION

Airport Architecture
by David Brodherson

In 1928, New York State Appellate Court Chief Judge Benjamin Cardoza wrote an influential opinion affirming the importance of municipal airports. In response to the City of Utica's bond issue to finance a new airport, taxpayer Albert O. Hesse sued to halt municipal airport development. Hesse believed that government development of airports was an inappropriate use of public money. Undeterred by a lower court's unanimous decision against him, he brought the case to the New York Court of Appeals on November 28, 1928. The eloquent Judge Cardoza, who later sat on the United States Supreme Court, explained:

> Aviation is today an established method of transportation. The future, even the near future, will make it still more general. The city that is without the foresight to build the ports for the new traffic may soon be left behind in the race of competition. Chalcedon was called the city of the blind, because its founders rejected the nobler site of Byzantium lying at their feet. The need for vision of the future in the governance of cities has not lessened with the years. The dweller within the gates, even more than the visitor from afar, will pay the price of blindness.[1]

These projects are huge investments of public and private commerce and industry, as well as symbols of architectural aspirations and urban pride. Denver's isolation on the frontier diminished in the 1860s when the Transcontinental Railroad crossed the country nearby to the north through Cheyenne, Wyoming, on a less costly traverse of the Rocky Mountains. In order to link Colorado to the rest of the country and end its frontier status, the State chartered a privately financed transcontinental line in 1870. Similarly, Denver International Airport bridges an aerial frontier functioning as a great gateway to the city, region and country.

Airports throughout the United States developed in four overlapping periods. Generally, the periods can be defined as 1926 to 1929, 1929 to 1941, 1945 to 1958 and 1958 onward. Airport architectural practice and theory, aviation public policy, aeronautical engineering in specific regard to aircraft size and type, the finance of airlines, and urban development and pride are among the factors determining these periods.

OPENING OF AMERICA'S FIRST AIR-RAIL PASSENGER TERMINAL. PAN AMERICAN AIRWAYS AIRPORT, MIAMI.

1

2

Architects designed the first passenger terminals in a formative, experimental era from 1926 to 1929. One type, a depot hangar, combined passenger facilities and airline offices in a modest building attached to a hangar. At Newark Airport in New Jersey, for example, the airlines began operating from a row of depot hangars. Gable and Wyant designed a depot hangar for Mines Field, which is now a cargo building at Los Angeles International Airport. The other predominant form, referred to as either the "simple terminal" or "administrative building," was akin to a modestly-sized and detailed railroad station, where passengers were processed in centralized, single-level areas with supplementary amenities and offices on upper levels. Evidence of this style is seen in the 1927 design of the Stout Air Services Terminal[2] at the Ford Airport in Dearborn, Michigan, and Miami's Pan-American Airways Terminal[3] built in 1928. The Austin Company's more elaborate "simple terminal", constructed in Burbank from 1929 to 1930, marked a transition into the second period.

During the second period, from 1929 to 1941, the simple terminal dominated. Urban planners, architects and civil engineers strove to create convenient, functional and symbolic gateways into central business districts. Despite the Great Depression, American cities built elaborate air transportation facilities. Although the great railroad depots of the world inspired the design of the overall structure, regional styles, such as Georgian and Spanish Colonial revivals and Art Deco, inspired many of the surface details. Some of the richest decorative programs, with references to aviation, were incorporated into functional elements. The standard ground level contained a waiting hall with an atrium, and was located at the intersection of a cruciform plan for centralized enplaning and deplaning passengers. The second level had balconies ringing the atrium while upper stories, with setbacks, housed air traffic control towers. Prominent examples of this type of architecture are the New Orleans Shoshun Airport[4] completed in 1933 and the marine and land-plane terminals[5] at LaGuardia built between 1938 and 1939.

1   Pan-American Airways Airport, Miami
2   LaGuardia Airport in New York

After World War II, local governments resumed development of airports in a third period from 1945 to 1958 and a fourth period from 1958 onward. Urbanization curtailed expansion at many existing airports during the third and fourth periods, forcing relocation to larger sites or additional facilities more distant from central business districts. This new airport transportation infrastructure includes Dallas-Fort Worth International, Washington Dulles International, Kennedy International and Chicago-O'Hare International airports.

From 1945 until 1958, construction of rectilinear International Style terminals with glass and steel or aluminum curtain walls became commonplace. The International Arrivals Building and the United Airlines Terminal[6] at Kennedy International Airport as well as O'Hare International Airport[7] are the most notable examples. Distinctive stone-riveted terminals in such cities as Pittsburgh, Houston and Seattle were the exception. Likewise, the expressionistic Trans World Airline Terminal[8] at Kennedy and the historicist Lambert St. Louis International Airport Terminal[9] were great exceptions to the proliferation of the International Style. While details referring to aviation largely disappeared, air traffic control towers began to emerge with oversized symbolic and functional details. The tower became a massive, iconic, sculptural, even expressionistic, separate building type—a "lighthouse in the air." Although constructed a few years after 1958, the air traffic control tower at LaGuardia Airport in New York attributed to Harrison and Abramovitz is an outstanding example.

During the fourth or current phase, architects began responding to the Post-Modern aesthetic. Most recently in this period, "hi-tech" streamlined aircraft forms and the demand for voluminous spaces inspired passenger terminals with exposed and decorative, curving steel trusses. The Washington National Airport[10], Kennedy International Airport's Terminal One[11] and the United Airlines Terminal[12] at O'Hare exemplify this trend. The Washington, D.C., Dulles International Airport[13] marks the transition into this exceptionally bold period by combining an indispensable suspension bridge and concrete technology into the structure.

1

2

1   Detail of control tower at Dulles International Airport
2   Detail of passenger circulation inside the Trans World Airlines' terminal at JFK Airport in New York
3   Detail of passenger circulation inside O'Hare Airport, Chicago, IL
4   United Airlines' concourse interior at O'Hare Airport, Chicago, IL

3

4

Terminals grew larger and were often separated into two components, both located near the center of the runway system: a linear airside concourse where aircraft waited, also referred to as a "remote satellite," and a landside building where passengers transfer to and from ground transportation. Similar to the New York City transit system, internal airport transportation systems with rubber-tired trains, light transit cars, moving walkways and mobile lounges akin to specially designed, oversized buses carry passengers over extremes of distance. Today such trains or moving walkways link landside and airside buildings or parking lots at international airports in Miami, Tampa, Newark, Pittsburgh, O'Hare, Atlanta, Las Vegas and most recently, Denver. Mobile lounges, originally created for Dulles International Airport, were also used elsewhere to ferry inbound international passengers and other passengers during rush hour.

The new Denver International Airport Passenger Terminal builds on the city's 60-year governmental commitment to commercial aviation. As in the era of rail, the Rocky Mountains initially barred an air route through Denver between the coasts. However, under the direction of Mayor Benjamin Stapleton, the City of Denver began planning a municipal airport in the late 1920s, a project *The Denver Post* labeled "Stapleton's Folly." H.S. Croker, an employee in the Parks Department, planned the 640-acre site. The airport opened in October 1929. The administration building was austerely detailed but well-massed. Despite the Great Depression, Denver Municipal Airport became an important hub by 1934. Renamed after Mayor Stapleton, the airport's expansion culminated in the late 1960s with a series of finger concourses and loading bridges designed by Denver architect Paul Reddy.

Discussion about the inadequacy of airport acreage at Stapleton Airport started as early as 1960. Between 1972 and 1989, a series of feasibility studies, plans and public hearings assessed the expansion of the existing airport, selection of a new airport location and advised upon both master and site plans. At the time of his election in 1983, Mayor Federico Peña preferred the expansion of Stapleton. However, within two years Mayor Peña concentrated upon a plan for construction of a new facility on land northeast of Denver.

In 1989, the City and County of Denver selected and commissioned Fentress Bradburn Architects to be the architects of the Passenger Terminal Complex at Denver International Airport. The design of and investment in this new airport was critical to Denver's image and commercial vigor. Just as the Denver Pacific Railroad and its depot were essential to Denver's growth from the terminus of a trunk line to a main line hub in the region and the country, in the 20th century Stapleton Airport helped stimulate the growth and awareness of Denver. The new fabric-roofed passenger terminal at Denver International Airport continues this heritage into the next century.

A combination of historicism, iconic acknowledgement of region and attention to technocratic demands distinguish this airport from others of the era. Much like the preceding urban transportation infrastructure, the approach to the terminal and its internal parti borrow from the ease of the Picturesque and the formal, grand drama of the Beaux-Arts. Both the massing of the roof and the interior details of the Great Hall refer to the great railroad stations of the late 19th century and early 20th centuries, and the airport terminals of the 1930s. For example, a mountain-like, translucent roof, supported on tall columns and spanning a great distance, creates the spacious Great Hall. A balcony above the main floor, reminiscent of airport architecture of the 1930s, lines the Great Hall allowing the recently arrived user to experience a vast space. Fentress Bradburn Architects has interpreted Jeppesen Sanderson aviation maps, still used by pilots as guides to individual airports, in the stone flooring at the north and south ends of the Great Hall.

The distinctive use of materials and forms from the environment and culture of the region surrounding the building creates a unique sense of place. In fact, the link between the mountains and the terminal's architectural image have become so strong that recently British Airways incorporated elements of architecture and landscape into its advertisements: umbrellas, symbolic of rainy weather, extend through the peaks of the airport roof in a light-hearted invitation to fly between London and Denver.

The role of aviation in Denver and other cities has far surpassed Chief Judge Cardoza's eloquent,

1

2

visionary 1928 opinion of the future of this mode of transportation. Indeed, Cardoza's opinion is as relevant now as it was seven decades ago: "The need for vision of the future in the governance of cities has not lessened with the years. The dweller within the gates, even more than the visitor from afar, will pay the price for blindness." Already the experiences of tens of millions of users, comments in the architectural, engineering and popular presses, and the commercial stimulus to the Rocky Mountain Region are a testament to the vision of architects and civic leaders. The new airport will help assure Denver's image as the Byzantium of the Rocky Mountains in the 21st century.

Notes

[1]Albert O. Hesse v. Fred J. Rath, as Mayor of the City of Utica, and Others, 224 New York Appellate Division Reports 344 – 346, 230 New York Supplement 676 – 679, Supreme Court of New York, Appellate Division, Fourth Department (1928); Hesse v. Rath, 249 New York Reports 436 – 438, 164 North Eastern Reporter 342 (Court of Appeals of New York 1928).

[2]Architect: Albert and Moritz Kahn

[3]Architect: Delano and Aldrich

[4]Architect: Weiss, Dreyfous and Seifurth

[5]Architect: Delano and Aldrich

[6]Architect: Skidmore, Owings and Merrill

[7]Architect: C.F. Murphy and Associates

[8]Architect: Eero Saarinen

[9]Architect: Hellmuth, Yamasaki and Leinweber

[10]Architect: Cesar Pelli and Associates

[11]Architect: Skidmore, Owings and Merrill

[12]Architect: Murphy/Jahn

[13]Architect: Eero Saarinen and Associates with engineers Ammann and Whitney

1   Stapleton International Airport in Denver
2   The new Denver International Airport in Denver

1

"IMAGINE A GREAT CITY"

1

For those who say we can't find the will to sacrifice now and invest in the future, I say, let them come to Denver. What you have done in Denver … is to roll up your sleeves and turn your dreams into reality. (Federico Peña, Mayor of Denver [1983 – 1991], U.S. Secretary of Transportation [1993 – 1996], "1991 to be a Year of New Beginnings and Strong Finishes," *Daily Journal,* 23 January 1991)

After the visionary Mayor Federico Peña was elected in 1983 with the campaign slogan, "Imagine a Great City," controversy surrounding Denver International Airport began in 1985 when he announced the new airport on Denver's horizon. The airport was lauded, and later proved to be the economic catalyst to push not only Denver, but also Colorado and many of the surrounding areas, to compete in national and international trade and commerce markets. An economic impact study produced by the Colorado Business Forum, a group of influential business leaders, was released in September 1986. It predicted that the new airport would generate 20,000 new jobs and $5.1 billion in business revenue.

In 1992, President Clinton commended Colorado for its strong record of job creation. He also stressed the direct correlation between the North American Free Trade Agreement (NAFTA) and a

boost in local export business. In fact, the University of Colorado at Boulder predicted that 24,100 net new jobs would be created for Colorado in 1993. Furthermore, a forecast released on October 22, 1993, by KPMG Peat Marwick predicted that Denver International Airport would generate nearly $40 million more in first-year revenues than the $353.6 million Leigh Fisher and Associates had predicted one year before. KPMG Peat Marwick anticipated a $30.5 million profit during Denver International Airport's first 12 months of operation, despite many construction delays and major cost overruns (Aldo Svaldi, "Profit Predicted for DIA: Forecast depends on traffic, concessions", *Denver Business Journal*, 29 October – 4 November, 1993).

In 1986, Denver's current airport, Stapleton International, was ranked as the fifth busiest airport in the nation, with over 34 million passengers and three major airline "hubs": United, Continental and Frontier. That same year, Stapleton-area residents filed a lawsuit because of noise issues, and the City affably settled the case with a guarantee to relocate the airport.

More importantly, two parallel north–south runways located too close to one another to simultaneously land planes during bad weather began causing major flight delays, which in turn affected the air traffic of the entire nation. "When

an adverse weather condition occurs, you get hammered, because it backs up the arrival rate in Denver … and that backs up the arrival rate all over the country," explained Airport Planner Richard Veazy (during a terminal planning, design and construction seminar on March 22, 1991 in Denver, Colorado, to the American Association of Airport Executives and the American Society of Civil Engineers). Mayor Peña soon announced that the project's timetable would be sped up in order to open in 1992, three years earlier than planned. Denver International Airport was projected to open in 1992 with six runways, 110 gates and the ability to serve 72 million people each year by the year 2000, making it the nation's second busiest airport, all with a price tag of $3 billion.

> First, Denver will be one of just a handful of major urban centers in the world with an uncongested airport. Second, Denver will have an airport with the capability of handling any type of aircraft going to any part of the globe. Given Denver's dependency on air transportation, this is critical. (George F. Doughty, City of Denver's Director of Aviation [1984 –1992], "What Denver International Airport Will Do for Denver is More Than Most Imagine," *Daily Journal*, vol. 97, no. 31, 7 July 1993)

1 View of Rocky Mountain range from the plains
2 Design sketch for the airport's initial roof concept

Airport officials and economic forecasters around the country used the two most recently built greenfield airports, Atlanta and Dallas-Fort Worth, completed nearly 20 years prior to Denver International Airport, as gauges by which to predict Denver International Airport's future. While their success may not be Denver's and vice versa, Dean Vanderbilt, President of the North Texas Commission designed to promote the Dallas-Fort Worth Airport, believes that the Dallas-Fort Worth Airport has clearly played a role in the area's economic success. A report by the Colorado Business Forum stated that:

> ... in both Dallas-Fort Worth and Atlanta, the most dramatic economic development has been the significant growth of international business. The link between international air service and the attraction of foreign capital and business development was repeatedly stressed by those interviewed. (Kurt Moeller, "Experts Say Future Rests on International Flights", *Wyoming Tribune-Eagle*, 1 December 1991, p. 3)

Moeller's article goes on to say that Denver International Airport's planning office released a report in 1986 stating that between 1975 and 1985, 816 new international businesses, an additional $3.3 billion in overseas capital and five-times as many international passengers had come into the area. Since the airport's opening in 1974, the immediate surrounding area doubled in population and experienced dramatic increases in tax revenue. Furthermore, the nearby town of Irving's population grew by 50% and tax revenue increased by $7.8 billion. Additionally, Dallas became one of the country's biggest centers for Fortune 500 companies' corporate headquarters.

In January 1991, then-Mayor Federico Peña optimistically spoke of Denver's future: "Denver is already regarded as one of the most livable cities in the United States. As we continue to build for the future, Denver will emerge as one of the most desirable places in North America to live, work, play and do business." The weak domestic and national economies of the late 1980s and early 1990s made it difficult for developers to find financing, even in Denver's strengthening economy. Nevertheless, many of the area's developers remained confident, intimating that the

quality and scale of Denver International Airport would end Denver's development freeze. Confidence radiated from developers such as Russ Waterson, partner in the ownership group of over 640-acres of the Gateway Area, who stated "that it will be such a spectacular facility that tongues will be wagging worldwide." This confidence was shared by Tucker Hart Adams, a prominent Denver economist and president of Adams Group, Inc., when she said that the decision to build Denver International Airport "is the single most important decision made in the State of Colorado in the last 100 years."

With an ever-growing population, the City and County of Denver, led by Mayor Peña, sought to create an iconic gateway for the economic growth of the city regionally, nationally and internationally. In order to create such a gateway for Denver, Fentress Bradburn Architects looked to emulate the characteristics that made the Sydney Opera House in Australia and the Eiffel Tower of Paris significant landmarks.

The airport was planned to be a world hub. In fact, with the North Pole as the center, an equilateral triangle between Tokyo, Frankfurt and Denver can be drawn with side lengths of only 6,000 miles. Expanding on the region's already visually powerful and highly publicized natural landmark, Fentress Bradburn Architects gained inspiration for the airport's roof structure in the geometric lines of the majestic Rocky Mountains' snow-capped peaks.

> Compared with most airports, this building feels good for the body. A walk along the main [terminal] beneath the trees that rise from the warm granite pavement is almost as pleasant as a mountain hike. The nature imagery evokes the reason Colorado draws new residents as well as tourists. (Herbert Muschamp, "A Wonder World in the Mile High City," *New York Times*, 7 May 1995, p. 34)

Curtis Fentress's initial design sketches for the Passenger Terminal Complex at Denver International Airport were far from his first attempt at defining the airport building form. While researching airport architecture for his college thesis, he observed that many pre-1960s airports

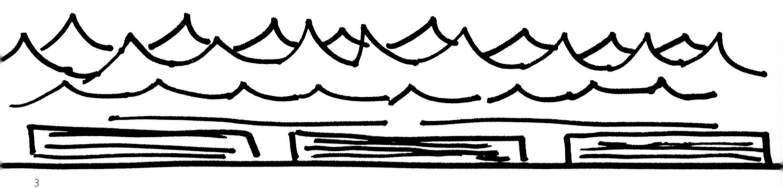

3

embodied the excitement born from the Wright brothers' launch of the first flying machine on December 17, 1903, at Kitty Hawk, North Carolina. He also noticed that in the past 35 years, the trend in airport architecture had been away from the needs of the user.

The demise of clear circulation paths, plus the lack of natural plant life, art and character have transformed the typical airport building type into the ultimate people processor, a "supermarket" characterized by a two-by-four ceiling grid, maze corridors, florescent lights, dark colors, low ceilings and a lack of natural light. Based on observations such as these, Fentress Bradburn Architects not only defined a vision for future airports, but also generated an overall design philosophy: "an artistic and scientific compilation of contextual regionalism and user-specificity within all aspects of building structure."

I envisioned a rejuvenation of the airport building through the incorporation of great spaces, along the lines of what took place with Grand Central Station. Passengers, the world over, are asking for airports to become more than people processors. I have found an opportunity to transfix the wonder and excitement of flight in the architecture of airports. (Curtis Fentress, Design Principal, Fentress Bradburn Architects Ltd.)

3　Concept design sketch

2

INNOVATIVE TEAMS AND PEOPLE

1

In an open and supportive environment, creative people make creative and innovative projects happen. (James Bradburn, Managing Principal, Fentress Bradburn Architects Ltd.)

The City and County of Denver's project management team, headed by William "Bill" Smith, coordinated over 10,000 people during the development and construction of Denver International Airport. Smith has had a long and illustrious career since receiving his first degree in geology from Colorado College. Before that, Smith entered the United States Army in 1958 as a draftee. Later, Smith attended the University of Colorado, where he graduated with a civil engineering degree in 1964. Smith began his career with the Denver Public Works Department. Mayor Peña promoted Smith to Associate Aviation Director in 1983. Smith then began to oversee airport expansion projects at Stapleton Airport. As Manager of Public Works, he also guided the construction at Denver International Airport. Wellington Webb, Mayor of Denver (1991 to present), properly credits Smith as "the person who, more than any single individual, was responsible for the construction of Denver International Airport."

William "Bill" Muchow, a Denver-area architect and an influential consultant, joined the City and County of Denver's airport construction team in early 1990. Muchow calmed much of the confusion among airport staff and designers by providing the architectural balance to the more engineering-oriented Smith.

Born in Denver, Muchow attended the University of Illinois and the Cranbook Academy of Art, where he received degrees in architecture before beginning his 50-year architectural career in Denver. Muchow's architectural practice designed over 800 projects starting in 1950. Muchow, a fellow of the American Institute of Architects, is often referred to as the "dean" of Denver

architects. His influence in the region was best described in a December 1982 *Daily Journal* article, which noted that "Muchow is probably the most widely known architect in the region, his name synonymous with consistent design excellence." Unfortunately, while both Smith and Muchow devoted invaluable time and energy to the Denver International Airport project, neither was able to see it to fruition: Muchow died in October 1991 and Smith died in October 1992.

Hana Rocek, Manager of Design, and Reginald Norman, Project Manager, were involved in work on the passenger terminal for the City and County of Denver. Both Norman and Rocek remain active in the Planning and Development departments at Denver International Airport. The City of Denver retained the joint venture of Greiner Engineering and Morrison-Knudsen Engineering (Greiner/MKE) as the project's Program Manager. All three entities formed the Program Management Team (PMT) together with key members of the City's Aviation Department. Richard Haury directed the Greiner/MKE joint venture, and William Seaver headed project costs. He also managed the overall and project-specific schedules with Ed Lett. Other significant members of the Greiner/MKE team were: Ron Thompson, who initially prepared the planning of the overall terminal complex and concourse configuration; Dick Holmgren, who monitored the architectural development of all facilities on the airport; and Bill McCoy as the terminal's Project Manager.

Mayor Peña's appointment of 15 Denver-area leaders to the Blue Ribbon Advisory Committee provided the Denver community with a direct avenue for feedback. The committee remained active for approximately two and a half years until Mayor Webb's election in 1991. Bob Albin, the initial proponent and longtime supporter of the new airport, served as chair, while Charles Ansbacher, director of the art program and special assistant to Director of Aviation, George Doughty,

1   Curtis Fentress and James Bradburn with roof
    model featuring a skylight

2

co-chaired and organized the committee as it strove to represent many facets of Colorado's citizens, including designers, community leaders and transportation personnel. The community's goals were kept in mind as the committee frequently met with consultants to discuss subjects such as parking, art, concessions, airlines, uniformity between the exterior and interior, signage, runway configuration, land use and design. It was often the committee's job to relate suggestions and concerns to Mayor Peña, Doughty and Smith. Encouraging airport officials to hear user concerns—an idea personally advocated by both Mayor Peña and Doughty—was unique in airport planning at the time.

The look and feel of the roof was a radical departure from any previous design presented. The fabric roof was lighter, requiring less from the structure beneath – a 'superstructure,' brilliantly planned. It is a tribute to Fentress Bradburn that they were able to present and pass the structure through Mayor Peña and Bill Smith. After all, it was everyone's goal for this billion-dollar facility

to have landmark qualities. What would make it have those qualities and represent our city? I believe Fentress Bradburn had the solution. (Charles Ansbacher, director of the art program and special assistant to Director of Aviation, George Doughty)

Fentress Bradburn Architects' in-house design and technical team collaborated with 27 consultants to create designs for the Passenger Terminal, the International Arrivals Building, the Airport Office Building, parking structures and approach roadways. Curtis Fentress as Design Principal and James Bradburn as Managing Principal orchestrated Fentress Bradburn Architects' involvement in the project. Michael Winters directed the architectural design effort, while Barbara Hochstetler Fentress directed the interior design effort. Design efforts on the North Terminal Support Area (NTSA), the Airport Office Building and future hotel (to insure proper foundation installation during the initial construction phase) were led by Brian Chaffee. Thom Walsh was hired for the Denver International Airport project because of his extensive work experience on

3

previous airports. He coordinated the overall effort as Project Manager and aviation specialist. Brit Probst filled the role of Project Administrator and Todd Britton coordinated the efforts of the model shop.

Except for Thom Walsh, these key in-house team members worked together on the one million-square-foot Colorado Convention Center project completed in 1990. This project was the most significant architectural undertaking by the City and County of Denver during the previous 30 years. Having attended over 100 public meetings on the Colorado Convention Center project with the mayor's office, city council and numerous public and private interest groups, Fentress Bradburn Architects team had the capacity, organization, continuity and attitude necessary to complete a project of this scope.

2   William E. Smith, Director of Pubic Works,
    City of Denver

3   Aviation Director Jim DeLong, with
    Mayor Wellington Webb in the background

COLLABORATION

On any given project, our goal is to establish an open and inviting environment where the free flow of ideas from intern to senior architect and citizen to client is not only encouraged but often integrated. This is the only way to ensure that the right idea for the project is found. (Curtis Fentress, Design Principal, Fentress Bradburn Architects Ltd.)

Perez and Associates were hired as the architects to work with Greiner/MKE on the early planning and programming concepts for the passenger terminal. When Fentress Bradburn Architects were commissioned as the architects for the Passenger Terminal Complex, the project was suffering from severe budgeting and scheduling over-runs. As a result, the first step in the year-long design process for Fentress Bradburn Architects was a three-week design charette aimed at solving both aesthetic and functional dilemmas. The team needed to meet both Mayor Peña's goal of creating a memorable and significant piece of civic architecture and Smith's goal of "generating a big box shape that could be hosed down at night, after the last flight and quickly made ready for the early morning flights." Issues that arose from early concepts were also addressed, redefining the internal workings of the building, while maintaining the master plan concept of the dual curbsides; this involved reworking both the vertical and horizontal circulation patterns, modifying the mechanical systems and altering access to the Automated Guideway Transportation System (AGTS).

The ability of Fentress Bradburn Architects' design team to find a solution that enhances the functional, box-shaped airport building form allowed the passenger terminal to develop into a landmark that makes the space exciting to be in, thereby enhancing the experience of the passenger. The Rocky Mountains provide a dramatic backdrop for the airport as it sits on the semi-arid plains 18 miles northeast of Denver. Motivation for the roof's shape, material and color stemmed from Fentress Bradburn Architects' desire to bring the Colorado outdoors inside. Congruency between exterior and interior is brought about by the fusion of two natural elements: form and light.

1

Fentress Bradburn Architects also analyzed the functional operations of the Passenger Terminal Complex's building systems and operations during the initial design charette, including their internal workings, circulation patterns, mechanical systems and the AGTS. The interior building systems were reorganized so that the mechanical equipment rooms were moved to a lower level for weight and scheduling reasons. Vertical cores with elevators and stairs, also developed as modules, were relocated to enhance the terminal structure's ability to resist wind loads. Circulation flows were simplified to allow the user to intuitively understand the space. Two passenger walkways were added in order to permit the user an immediate understanding of the organization by providing a clear vista to the security pavilions, arrivals areas and the AGTS. In addition, these walkways allowed for less congestion in the central area of the Great Hall.

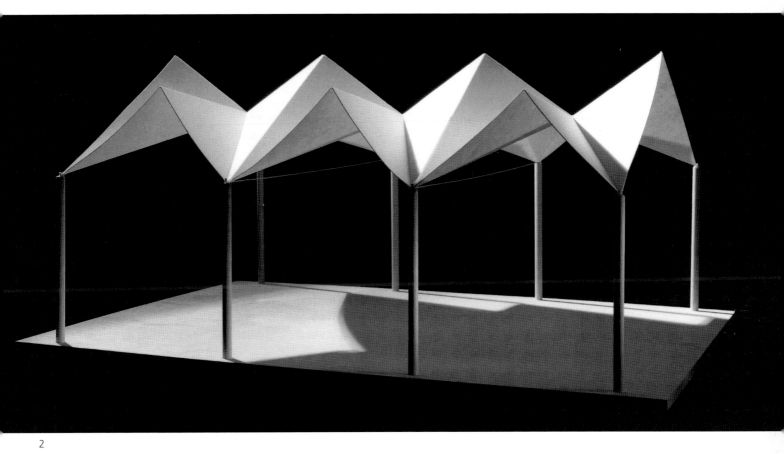

2

The design phase involved numerous meetings. From informal hallway meetings to elaborate presentations, the project's continuity demanded regular attendance of the City of Denver's Project Manager, Reginald Norman, and Fentress Bradburn Architects' Project Manager, Thom Walsh. Senior members from the core design team also retained an active role during the project in order to maintain a high-degree of efficiency that provided quick, comprehensive and creative design solutions.

Design Team Organization

Owner
City and County of Denver

Curtis W. Fentress
Design Principal
James H. Bradburn
Managing Principal

Thomas J. Walsh
Project Director
Michael O. Winters
Design Director

Project Architect Airport Office Building	**Pouw Associates** Structured Parking	**Project Architect** Terminal	**Project Architect** Internat'l Arrivals Building	**Project Controls** Manager

CAD   CAD   CAD

Project Design Coordinator

AOB Team	**Parking Team**	**Terminal Team**	**IAB Team**	**Q.A. Staff**
Civil	Transportation	Civil	Civil	Estimators
Interior Design	Civil	Landscape	Interior Design	V.E. Staff
Structural	Structural	Interior Design	Structural	Schedulers
Mechanical	Mechanical	Structural	Mechanical	Clerks
Electrical	Plumbing	Mechanical	Electrical	Bookkeepers
Plumbing	Lighting	Electrical	Plumbing	
Lighting	Signage	Plumbing	Lighting	
Acoustics	Graphics	Lighting	Acoustics	
Curtain Wall	Elevator	Acoustics	Curtain Wall	
Signage	Security	Curtain Wall	Signage	
Graphics	Air Quality	Signage	Graphics	
Elevator/Escalator	Fire and Life Safety	Graphics	Elevator/Escalator	
Telephone	Geotechnical	Elevator/Escalator	Moving Walks	
Security	Roofing	Moving Walks	Telephone Page	
Air Quality		Telephone Page	Security	
Fire and Life Safety		Security	Transportation	
Geotechnical		Transportation	Air Quality	
		Air Quality	Food Service	
		Food Service	Airlines	
		Airlines	Wind & Snow	
		Wind & Snow	Fire and Life Safety	
		Fire and Life Safety	Geotechnical	
		Geotechnical	Daylight	
		Daylight	Roofing	
		Roofing		

3

1   Photo of Fentress Bradburn Architects' employees
2   Early model study of possible roof structure
3   Design team organization chart

1

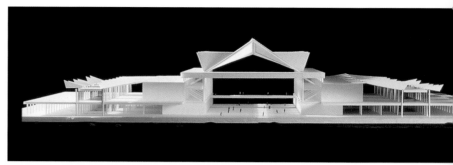

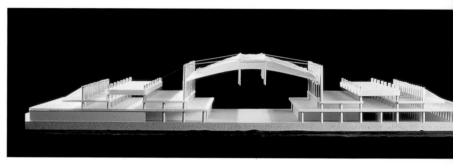

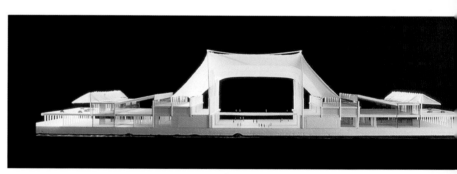

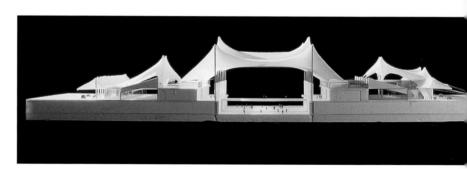

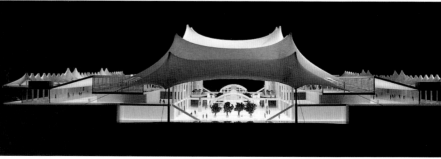

A comprehensive effort was maintained from design development through construction completion by means of weekly all-day Friday team meetings in which the core design team met with specialized consultants. Friday mornings began with an evaluation of the progress being made from one week to the next. Different design phases of the project were chronologically reviewed and critiqued through the use of diagrams and cardboard models. This process lent continuity to the project as work shifted from the exterior inward, and also helped resolve design and technical issues simultaneously. For example, discussions over programming issues such as security location, or modifications to the ticketing area were led by those designers actively involved in that specific issue, from senior architects to intern architects. Status reports were extremely accurate, and the schedule remained on target due in a large part to the consistent attendance of senior team members, including Curtis Fentress, James Bradburn, Michael Winters, Brian Chaffee, Thom Walsh, Barbara Hochstetler Fentress and Brit Probst.

After lunch, the core design team began individual meetings with specialized consultants. Mechanical, electrical and structural consultants and occasionally civil engineers were often present for the duration of the afternoon, while consultants in such specialties as acoustics (Shen Milsom Wilke) and baggage (TRA) were sequenced for efficiency purposes. In addition, Western Industrial Contractors moved into Fentress Bradburn Architects' office as the project's in-house estimators. They were available for cost and scheduling needs, and to assess the overall status of the team.

2

3

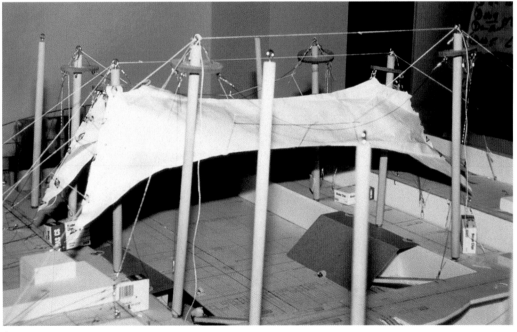

4

1 Fentress Bradburn Architects' design studio

2 Series of conceptual roof structure models

3&4 Photos of phasing models for fabric roof installation

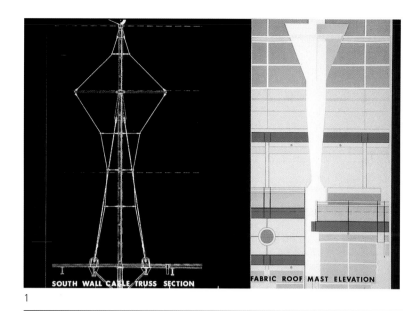

SOUTH WALL CABLE TRUSS SECTION

FABRIC ROOF MAST ELEVATION

1

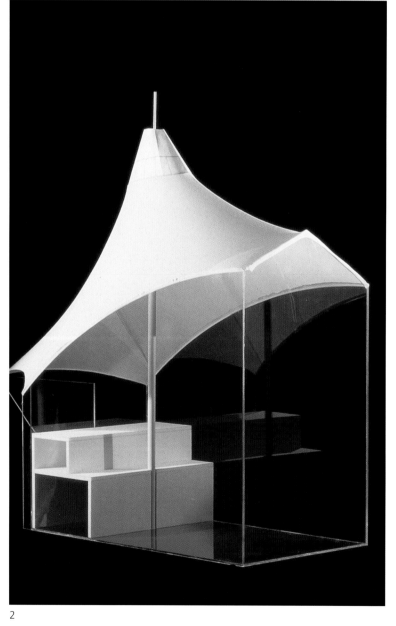

2

NORTH BUILDING ELEVATION

PARTIAL EAST ELEVATI

EAST / WEST BUILDING ELEVATI

3

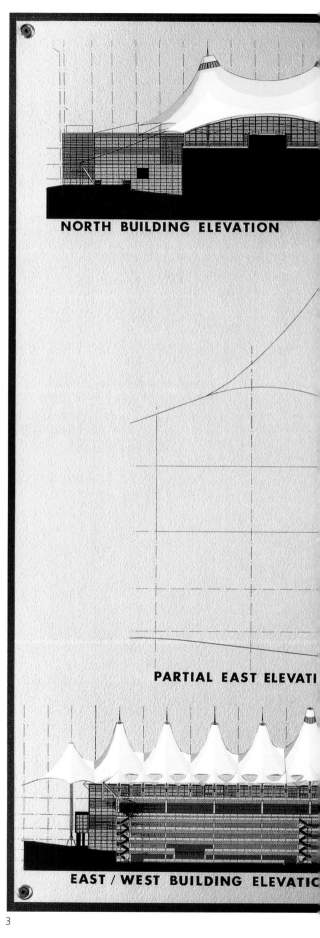

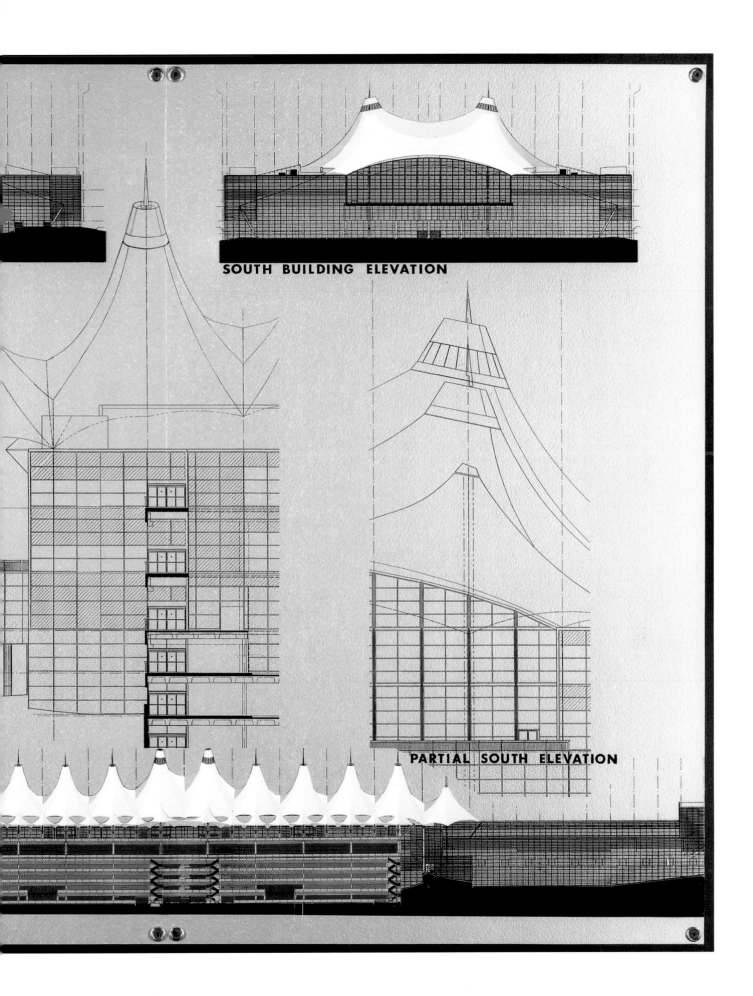

SOUTH BUILDING ELEVATION

PARTIAL SOUTH ELEVATION

1 South wall cable truss section and fabric roof mast elevation
2 Detail model of fabric roof peak
3 Series of building elevations

1
2
3
4
5

The idea was that if you could get the entire project team, both design and technical members, to attend brainstorming sessions, it made it easier to proceed with a solution that we were confident would solve the challenges – [this] eliminated a post-design dialogue. Based on the way that the passenger terminal complex turned out, I think you could see that not much changed from the initial design concept drawings all the way through, because everyone had an idea why it was the way it was. I also think that the technical groups felt ownership in the design, and in that respect it bolstered more of a team spirit. (Thom Walsh, Director of Airports, Fentress Bradburn Architects Ltd.)

During the construction phase, Friday team meetings were also used as a vehicle for discussing the progress made over the previous week and the progress to be expected during subsequent weeks. However, much of the focus centered on impending owner-requested changes. For example, the addition of a flow-through baggage system at United Airlines ticket counters caused numerous structural design changes within the building, and re-specification and redesign for curbside baggage devices.

To maintain communication and progress on all areas of the project, discussions surrounding challenging areas were phased through multiple meetings. Numerous owner changes mandated 96 additional services and three amendments (the International Arrivals Building, Airport Office Building and parking garage expansion) to Fentress Bradburn Architects' contract. Issues, such as relocating the rental car desks from level one to level five, began to arise and demanded immediate responses from the field team. Friday team meetings allowed a fairly fluid communication between the field team and the office team. Overall, this project stands as an excellent example of how continuous teamwork produces an amazingly seamless design.

Fentress Bradburn Architects utilized their own in-house model shop, consisting of six personnel led by Todd Britton, on every phase of the project, including: models of form, interior design, daylighting, skylights and interior spaces, overall site erection, curbside and parking structure, maquettes of walls, security pavilions and ticket counters. The importance of using models on a project of this magnitude goes well beyond benefiting the design team. Models also aid the public process by simplifying abstract ideas into

6

8

7

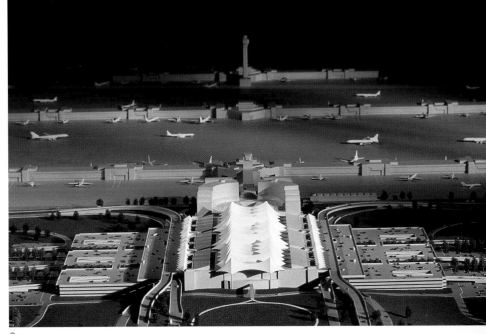

9

10

1&4 Model photo detail of ticketing hall
clerestories, curbside canopies and roof peaks
2&3 Model photo detail of curbside drop-off levels
5 Model photo detail of south-end curtain wall
6–10 Aerial photos of master plan model

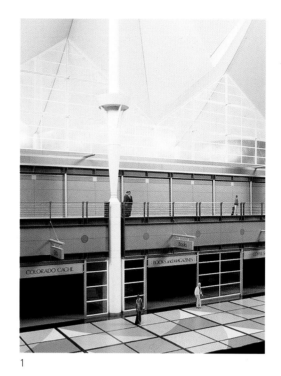

1

2

presentation models for laypersons and public officials. Close relationships were also fostered between the designers and the model-makers, facilitated by an in-house model shop and the ability to relay drawings electronically from designer to model-makers.

Simultaneously with Fentress Bradburn Architects' effort, the City and County of Denver held its own weekly meetings covering many of the same issues such as newly arisen problems, challenging upcoming areas, etc. In addition, monthly partnering sessions occurred at the site throughout the construction phase with senior management from the City of Denver, the project management team, contractors and Fentress Bradburn Architects. Partnering sessions allowed each of the parties involved to feel that project challenges would be resolved on a win–win basis.

The Passenger Terminal Complex sits on the frontier of airport architecture because of Fentress Bradburn Architects' determination to hear the individual needs of the airport's public, private and owner interest groups. Through numerous meetings and reports, Fentress Bradburn Architects defined the overall objectives of these groups to be the creation of: a functionally and aesthetically innovative design; a building responsive to the needs of all user groups; an example of civic architecture and pride; and a building to establish Denver as a major gateway to regional, national and global markets.

3

1&2 Model photos of concessions
  3 Model photo of ticketing counters
  4 Partnership agreement
  5 Model photo of west side of passenger terminal

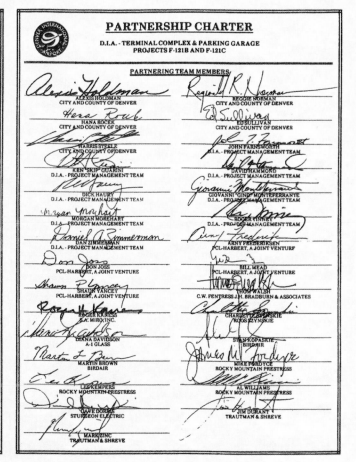

PARTNERSHIP CHARTER

DENVER INTERNATIONAL AIRPORT
TERMINAL COMPLEX & PARKING GARAGE
PROJECTS F-121B AND F-121C

We, the members of this Partnering Team, are committed to working together
in a spirit of ...

***TRUST, RESPECT, MUTUAL UNDERSTANDING, INTEGRITY,
OPEN COMMUNICATION, TEAMWORK, RESPONSIBILITY,
ACCOUNTABILITY AND PROMOTION OF THE HIGHEST LEVEL OF CREATIVITY***

and, we do hereby commit corporately and individually
to the following goals ...

** PRIDE IN BUILDING A QUALITY, LANDMARK PROJECT.
** NO ACCIDENTS.
** NO LITIGATION.
** CONVEY PARTNERING & TRUSTING RELATIONSHIPS TO TEAM PLAYERS AT ALL
   LEVELS.
** ALL PARTNERS MAKING A FAIR PROFIT AT THE LEAST COST TO
   THE CITY & COUNTY OF DENVER.
** CREATE AN ENJOYABLE WORKING ENVIRONMENT.
** COMPLETE PROJECT ON/OR AHEAD OF SCHEDULE & ON/OR UNDER BUDGET.
** BE A PARTNERING MODEL FOR THE INDUSTRY.

WILLIAM E. SMITH
CITY AND COUNTY OF DENVER

GORDON D. RUSSELL
PCL-HARBERT, A JOINT VENTURE

GINGER EVANS
CITY AND COUNTY OF DENVER

JAMES H. BRADBURN
C.W. FENTRESS J.H. BRADBURN & ASSOCIATES

PAT STRICKLIN
D.I.A. PROJECT MANAGEMENT TEAM

PARTNERSHIP CHARTER

D.I.A. - TERMINAL COMPLEX & PARKING GARAGE
PROJECTS F-121B AND F-121C

PARTNERING TEAM MEMBERS

ALEXIS HOLDMAN
CITY AND COUNTY OF DENVER

REGGIE NORMAN
CITY AND COUNTY OF DENVER

HANA ROCEK
CITY AND COUNTY OF DENVER

ED SULLIVAN
CITY AND COUNTY OF DENVER

HARRIS STEELE
CITY AND COUNTY OF DENVER

JOHN FARNSWORTH
D.I.A. - PROJECT MANAGEMENT TEAM

KEN "SKIP" GUARINI
D.I.A. - PROJECT MANAGEMENT TEAM

DAVID HAMMOND
D.I.A. - PROJECT MANAGEMENT TEAM

DICK HAURY
D.I.A. - PROJECT MANAGEMENT TEAM

GIOVANNI "GINO" MONTEFERRANTE
D.I.A. - PROJECT MANAGEMENT TEAM

MORGAN MOREHART
D.I.A. - PROJECT MANAGEMENT TEAM

ROGER VINNEY
D.I.A. - PROJECT MANAGEMENT TEAM

DAN ZIMMERMAN
D.I.A. - PROJECT MANAGEMENT TEAM

ARNY FREDERIKSEN
PCL-HARBERT, A JOINT VENTURE

DON JOSS
PCL-HARBERT, A JOINT VENTURE

BILL MEAD
PCL-HARBERT, A JOINT VENTURE

SHAUN YANCEY
PCL-HARBERT, A JOINT VENTURE

THOM WALSH
C.W. FENTRESS J.H. BRADBURN & ASSOCIATES

ROGER RAMESS
S.A. MIROX INC.

CHARLETTE BRODSKIE
ROOSZYNSKIE

DIANA DAVIDSON
A-1 GLASS

STAN KOPASKIE
BIRDAIR

MARTIN BROWN
BIRDAIR

MIKE FORDYCE
ROCKY MOUNTAIN PRESTRESS

LEE KEMPERS
ROCKY MOUNTAIN PRESTRESS

AL WILLIAMS
ROCKY MOUNTAIN PRESTRESS

DAVE DORRIS
STURGEON ELECTRIC

JIM DURANT
TRAUTMAN & SHREVE

MARK ZINC
TRAUTMAN & SHREVE

4
CREATIVE ELEMENTS

1

Architecture is about light and how it is used within a space. What is special about this design is that it is simple and elegant. (Bill Muchow, independent architectural consultant to the City and County of Denver on Denver International Airport)

Daylighting and Tensile-Membrane Roof
Fentress Bradburn Architects led the core design team of Lam Associates, Severud Associates (with Horst Berger), Rowan, Williams, Davies and Irwin, Shen Milsom Wilke, Black and Veatch and the Architectural Energy Corporation from the design charette that suggested the Teflon-coated fiberglass tensile-membrane roof through its construction. The ultimate challenge for this team was to structurally capture the striking roof profile and sculptural form of Fentress's first concept sketch. This design is much more than simply a rejection of airport architecture during the last 30 years; it also marks a movement toward defining an airport as something greater than it had ever been viewed as before—an expression of the region and an answer to the needs of the user.

As we were looking at possible structural systems and roof materials, Jim Bradburn suggested that the most efficient solution for spanning the space, especially with the form being considered, was a lightweight cable and fabric structure. (Curtis Fentress, Design Principal, Fentress Bradburn Architects Ltd.)

2

1 Early concept renderings of exterior structure
2 East elevation rendering
3 Cross section illustrating the effects of daylighting

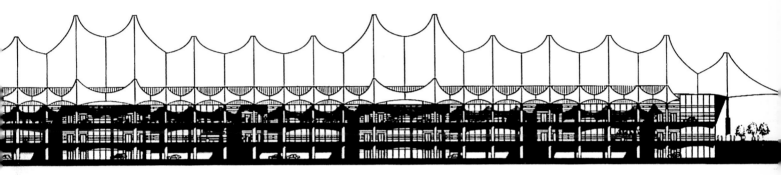

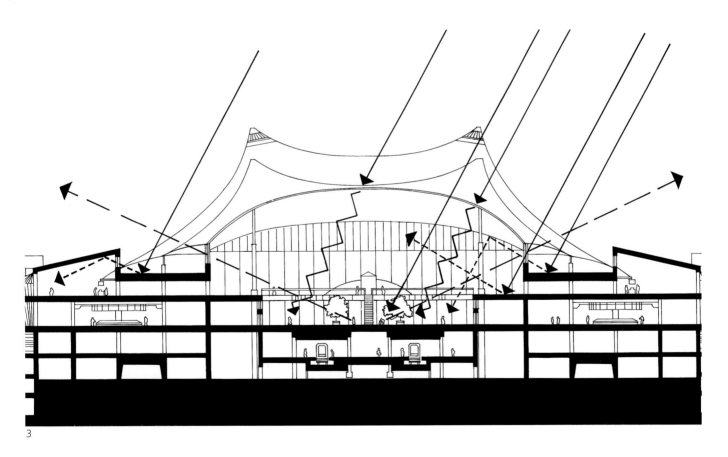

3

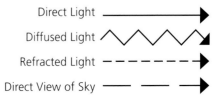

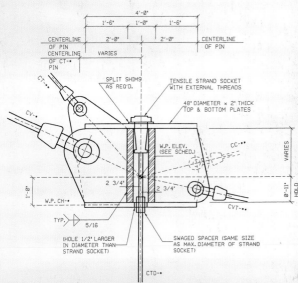

2

The design team began by investigating the use of steel, concrete and fabric as possible roofing materials. A couple of days into the design charette, James Bradburn contacted Horst Berger for his expertise on fabric roofs. Bradburn found that Berger had recently rejoined Severud Associates, a collaborator with Fentress Bradburn Architects on Denver's 1999 Broadway Building 10 years earlier.

Collaboration with Severud, engineer of record for the Teflon-coated fiberglass tensile-membrane roof of the passenger terminal, began a week into the design charette with the arrival of Berger. Berger, with colleagues Mark Schlogel and Ed DePaola, supplied the team with a wealth of knowledge about what was possible with fabric structures, and how to adapt a fabric structure to meet the overlapping climatic, aesthetic and functional requirements of the passenger terminal.

Engineers from Severud tested several different alternatives by developing computerized images of the various roof profiles. It soon became apparent that the team's wealth of knowledge would enable the original design sketches to be achieved. The geometry of these structures is not arbitrary. Once the parameters have been determined, "There is only one three-dimensional surface shape under which the structure is in equilibrium at all points," according to Berger.

A simple and direct approach, consisting of two rows of 17 masts matching the length of the Great Hall, held in place by two sets of primary cables,

Opposite:
   Airport Office Building with detail of
   "octopus connection"

2 Detail drawing of "octopus connection"

1

2

allowed the 1,000-foot-long roof to be sectioned into thirds, which facilitated a taller roof area over the conjoining bridges. The problem of connecting the cables of the tie-down anchors, valley cables, edge catenaries and downward and outward cables to each other was solved with Ed DePaola's "octopus connection."

In an effort to determine that the structure was buildable, Fentress Bradburn Architects' model shop began to develop a number of test models using simple wood dowels to support jersey material. As the need for further test models arose, fabric manufacturers supplied information about

1&2 Alternative roof structure study models
3 Model of Great Hall interior
4 Fabric roof mast section with skylight

3

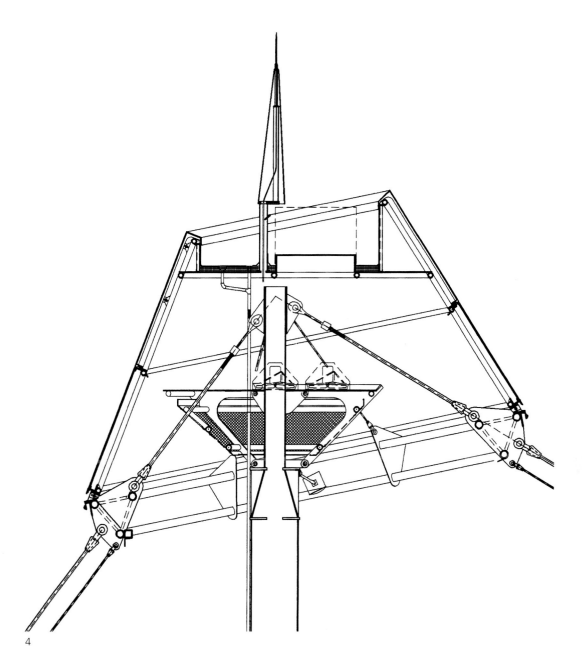

4

fabrication, erection, size of components and constructability. As James Bradburn, Managing Principal, said at the time:

> Each day the design is becoming more tangible. The anticipation of travelers arriving in Denver, welcomed by an interior space of dignified form and daylight, is becoming a reality.

Additional aesthetic challenges arose as the architects and Blue Ribbon Advisory Committee adamantly supported the inclusion of natural light throughout the space. Colorado's quality of light and vistas are enhanced at Denver International Airport through the inclusion of clerestories, skylights and the grandness of the Great Hall roof structure, while passenger flow and organization are simplified in a rectilinear building form. Due to structural reasons, many design team engineers protested the inclusion of skylights and clerestories. The transparent qualities of fabric

roofing helped to reduce the number of skylights and clerestories, while the clerestories lining the edge of the Great Hall remained as a buffer between the rigid walls and the flexible roof. The south-end curtain wall, the clerestories above the ticketing area and the skylights atop the tallest peaks endured through the collaboration process. Fentress Bradburn Architects' design team remained adamant about their inclusion, and defined them as an indicator of the weather outdoors, the time of day and the only source by which to bring in direct sunlight to animate the space.

> While sharing with the cathedral builders of the past the spirit of turning construction technology into art, everything else about this structure points to an architectural future as advanced as the planes it serves. The result is a space of great simplicity, clarity and visual diversity ... Nothing about its form is arbitrary, and its visual strength derives directly from

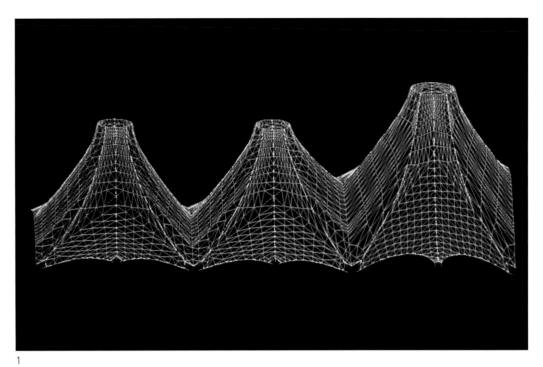

1

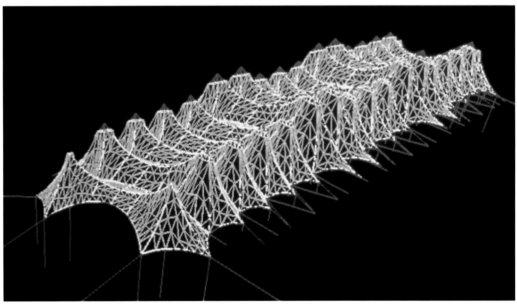

2

the expression of the force flow in the structure. (Horst Berger, Principal Engineer of the fabric roof, Severud Associates)

The functional aspects of utilizing a fabric roof, as opposed to a conventional roof, are most apparent from a structural standpoint. At two pounds per square foot, the lightweight and flexible qualities of a Teflon-coated fiberglass tensile-membrane roof eliminated 300 tons of steel and 200,000 linear feet of concrete shear wall from the early concept plan. The structure, in part because of its aerodynamic design, is able to absorb pressure from high winds and transfer it through the Great Hall floor system, resolving the force in the earth.

Climatic concerns centered on how the fabric roof would react to wind and snow. Rowan, Williams, Davies and Irwin (RWDI), special wind and snow consultants, who Fentress Bradburn Architects had worked with on the 1999 Broadway office tower in downtown Denver, engaged Dr. Peter Irvin to conduct snow load and wind tunnel tests. To determine the fabric roofing's reaction to snow accumulation, grains of sand, simulating snow, were added to a water solution containing a roof model. Wind currents were also introduced using artificially propelled sand in water to simulate the meteorological data collected over the previous 20 years. Snow loads of eight feet and deformations of 30 inches formed when the roof was subjected to snow loads of 80 pounds per square foot. The design was modified to alleviate these conditions.

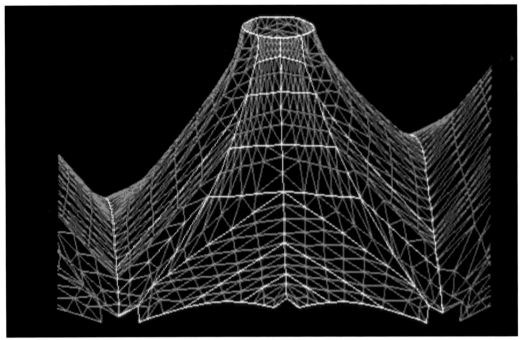

3

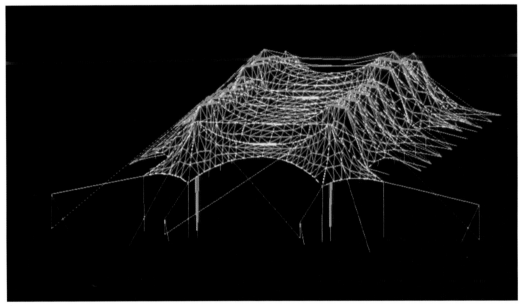

4

Fabric structures remain one of the most maintenance-free roofing systems for large commercial structures. Prior experience by Birdair from over 15 million square feet of installations indicates that maintenance generally consists of periodic inspections and cleaning. When a repair is needed, hand-held equipment is used to weld a new layer over the damaged area using a co-polymer of the Teflon coating. This fabric roofing system is the only major structure and enclosure system to carry a 20-year warranty, coupled with an ongoing maintenance commitment by its fabricator. Owners and operators of other major facilities with this roofing system report that such systems require considerably less maintenance time and expense than conventional roofing systems.

1–4   Computer generated roof models

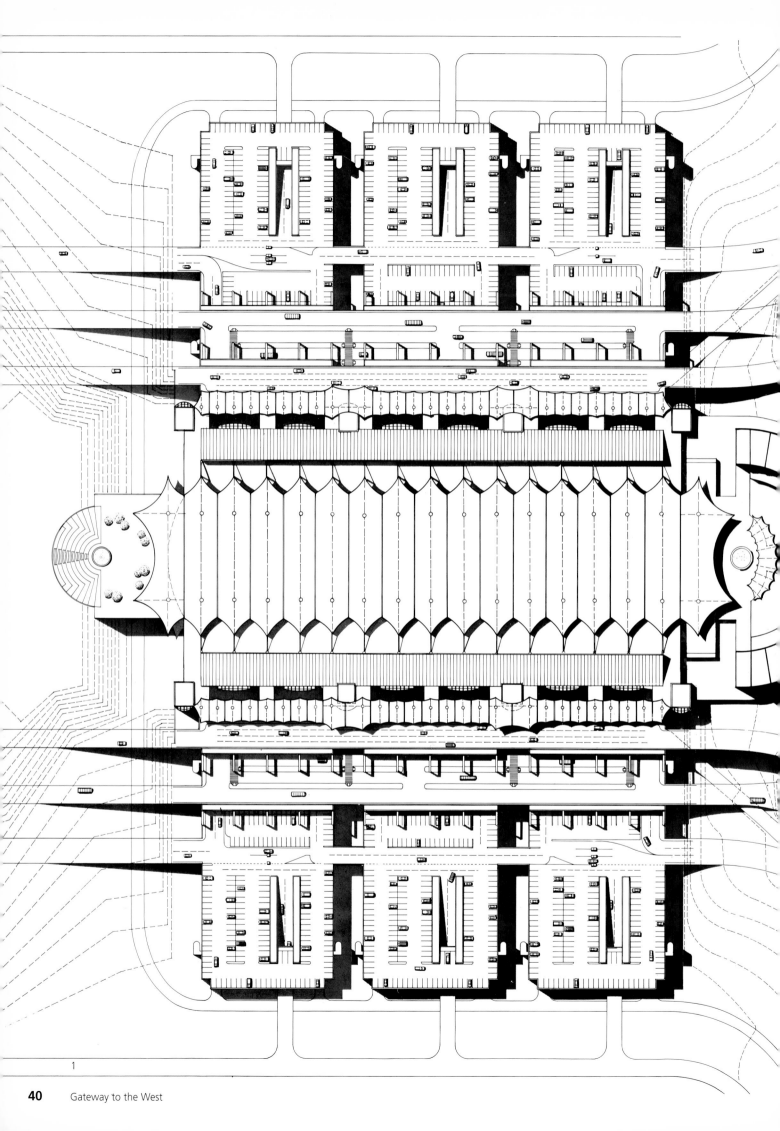

1

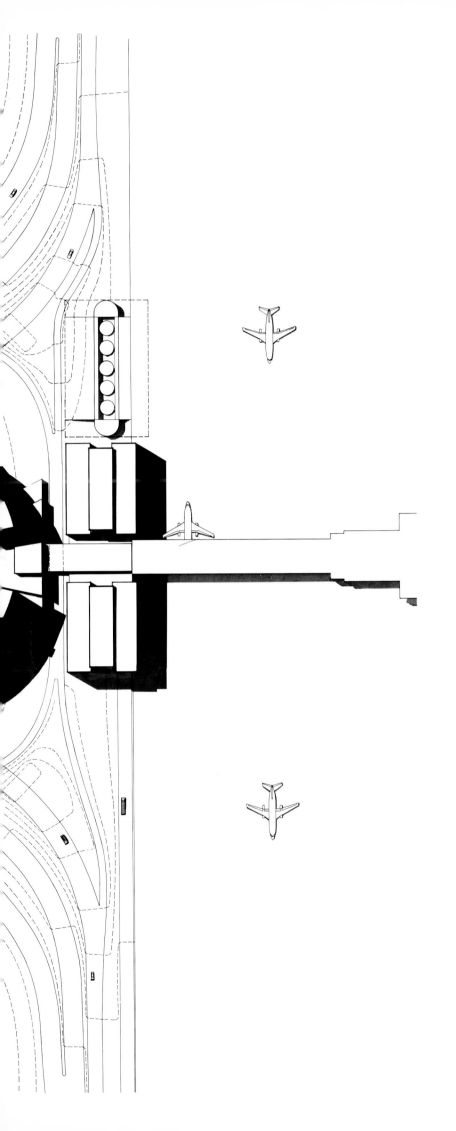

1   Roof plan of Passenger Terminal Complex

Following page:
2   Ticketing counters with granite flooring

2

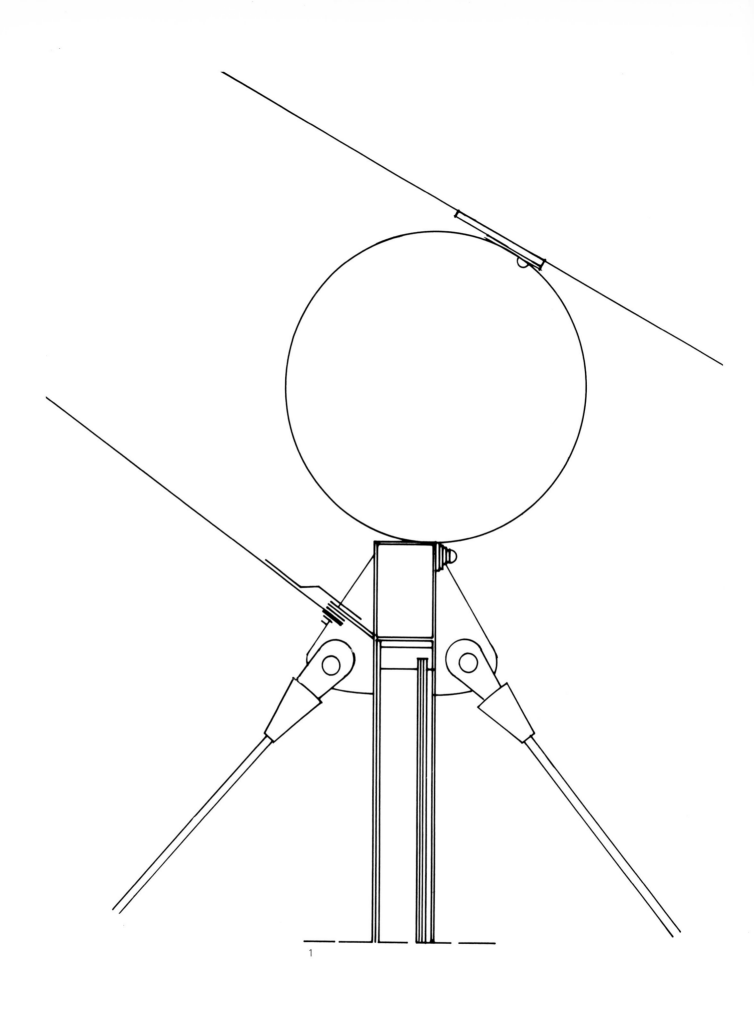

1   Detail of "sausage connection"

The direct and indirect lighting from the fabric roof and clerestories allows for minimal use of artificial lighting, which is both an energy consumer and heat producer, during daytime hours. The fabric reflects 40% of all incident solar radiation landing on its surface. Due to its low thermal mass, it does not heat up nor radiate heat into the space below like most conventional roofing systems. Thus, the space's cooling requirements are significantly lessened. As Michael Holtz of Architectural Energy Corporation pointed out:

> If daylighting can provide the majority of ambient lighting for the atrium, ticketing, baggage claim, and circulation spaces during the day, the simultaneous demand from the peak cooling load and full electric lights can be avoided.

In addition, energy costs are minimized and there are fewer operational problems because of the use of timed photocell controls.

Holtz also explained that the decision not to include insulation between the two layers of fabric, which would save an average of $48,000 per year in energy costs, was decided after results from several test models came back. These models indicated that: it would be very difficult to maintain quality control during installation; there was a strong potential for insulation to move over time; moisture damage was likely due to condensation; fabric roof manufacturers recommended against insulation, based on past project experience; and most importantly, daylight would not penetrate the roof as easily.

Computer-generated analyses utilizing models provided by the Department of Energy (DOE-2) and the American Society of Heating, Refrigerating and Air Conditioning Engineers (ASHRAE 90.1) were also performed. Results showed that the building envelope was not a critical contributing element of the building's energy usage, unlike the internal elements, such as people, computers, cathode ray tubes (CRTs), baggage handling equipment, lighting and mechanical building systems. Based on these results, part of the design team's effort was focused on minimizing these energy impacts.

Holtz also highlighted additional energy-efficient system design concepts that make Denver's airport one of the most energy-efficient airport structures in the world. In order to optimize benefits from daylighting, a low-E insulating glass was used on the perimeter exposures to reduce both heat gain and loss. In addition, perimeter clerestories in the baggage claim and ticketing areas were glazed. An eight-module design of the heating, ventilation and air conditioning (HVAC) systems divides service into six areas allowing discontinued service or reduced service to any unoccupied or temporarily unleased areas. Energy needed for winter heating is reduced through waste recovery in the baggage area make-up ventilation systems. Hot water heating is localized to reduce heat loss in distribution and eliminate re-circulation pumping energy. Lastly, highly energy-efficient motors, luminaries, lamps and ballasts have been utilized throughout the facility.

Daylighting, through the Teflon-coated fiberglass membrane structure and clerestories, virtually eliminated the use of artificial lighting during daylight hours. By creating high-volume public spaces, Fentress Bradburn Architects utilized the mechanical concept of stratification: hot air rises and cool air falls. Air conditioning is introduced only on lower levels where people are located, and as the air becomes heated, it rises into the space above. Traditionally, this air needs to be re-introduced into the mechanical system in order to return it to its conditioned state, but since the fabric roof has relatively little mass, the roof acts exothermically, allowing the dissipation of heat.

Design of the roof structure allows for an interplay of structural forces. Some challenging opportunities arose because the structure is so dynamic: the tops of the masts can move as much as two feet in any direction. Innovative solutions were required to fasten the fabric to the rigid building structure. First, the design of the glass walls needed to be addressed. Cantilevering the walls, using cable elements and bow trusses from the floor structure, allowed the connection between roof and wall to be discontinuous. These trusses are both vertical and horizontal to ensure the stability of the wall and allow independence from the roof. This system was utilized on the north and south walls with vertical cantilevers of 50 and 70 feet, and on the 30-foot clerestories that skirt the 1,000-foot Great Hall space.

Cantilevered walls terminate approximately two feet below the exterior fabric-roof structure where a flexible weather barrier provides a seal between the top of the glass wall and the underside of the inner layer of the fabric roof. After researching several options, a pliable two-foot diameter vinyl tubular section, nicknamed the "sausage connection," was selected. The tubular section remains inflated, keeping it from resting on the interior roof membrane, or draping over the glass's exterior. After the tube is attached to the fabric roof, a fin is inserted and mechanically fastened in the top glazing rabbet. Air release valves line the exterior face allowing air to escape during dramatic vertical and horizontal roof movement.

Due to Colorado's elevation and geographical location, ultra violet (UV) degradation is an issue that required extra consideration to the exterior building materials. Teflon was found to be naturally impervious to UV degradation based on test results comparing a sample from a current run of fabric with 19-year old fabric. Additionally, independent tests identified no discernable degradation between the new and old samples of fabric.

The new fabric was also subjected to several tests for noise control under controlled laboratory conditions. One such test involved a computer model representing the actual distance from the passenger terminal to the closest runway, direction of the aircraft, type of aircraft, noise source and other important characteristics. This computer model was designed to simulate the actual sound pressure that could be expected from an aircraft taking off. Together with other published data, these tests were compared to actual field test results at Vancouver's Canada Harbor Place Convention Center, a similar installation. Test results were corroborated within three decibels, well within the established federal acoustical performance criteria. The anticipated levels of noise within the terminal allow normal speech conversation and public address systems to perform as needed.

1

2

3

4

1   Interior design presentation board
2   Collaboration session on interior design
3&4   Interior design presentation boards

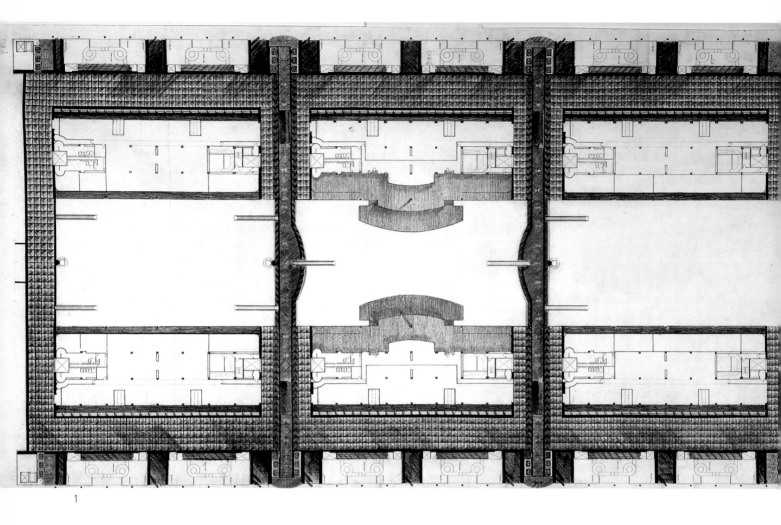

1

Functional concerns, including aesthetic values and adherence to budget and schedule, coupled with the areas addressed above, convinced Bill Smith initially and then the Blue Ribbon Advisory Committee that the Teflon-coated fiberglass tensile-membrane roof structure not only met but exceeded its expectations. As Curtis Fentress explains:

> ... our strength lies in our ability to create [a project] anew every time, to remain in the confines of the contemporaneous, to communicate ideas to an audience that is very much aware of what it is to exist now, [and] to be intuitive.

Fentress specializes in innovative aesthetic design, while Bradburn's specialty lies in technical innovation. This unique collaboration led the way to the design and construction of an icon: the Teflon-coated fiberglass tensile-membrane structure, whose fabric utilizes state-of-the-art, energy-efficient technology to cover a long, expansive space. The exterior's earthy-toned precast provides contrast to the futuristic brushed stainless steel columns and wall panels. Attention to both exterior and interior details expresses to users a genuine care for their well-being.

Interiors

By emulating the Colorado Rocky Mountains, the floor patterns and architectural canopies reinforce the form of the terminal. The technology of the roof is carried into the design of the passenger terminal's millwork and light canopies. (Barbara Hochstetler Fentress, Director of Interior Design [1986 – 1993], Fentress Bradburn Architects Ltd.)

Barbara Hochstetler Fentress and the interior design team worked with the overall theme of the building and futuristic technology. The color palette is based on Colorado's unique and distinctive environment. Coherence between exterior and interior is maintained by allowing the granite of the flooring to be directly representative of the natural local surroundings.

Granite with shades of white and deeper rust tones was utilized in four different shades to achieve a greater depth within the pattern. Black grid patterns accent this depth by providing definition and continuity throughout the facility. As Hochstetler Fentress states, such patterns are "like silhouettes in nature." This floor pattern, found throughout the terminal, reinforces the "mountainous" roof structure while also directing

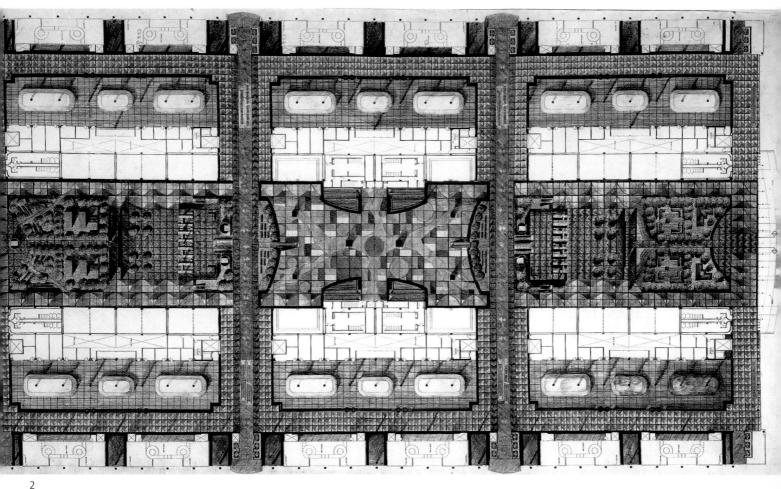

2

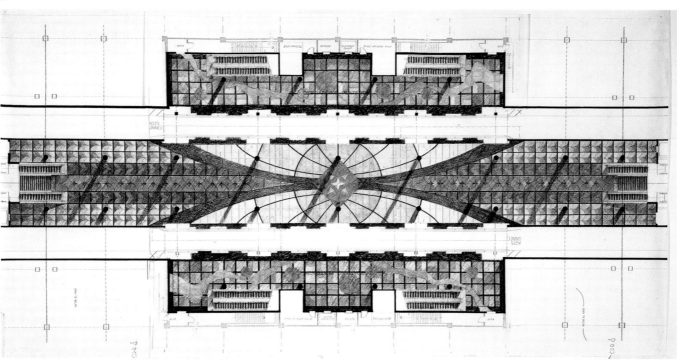

3

1   Sixth level interior granite floor pattern drawing
2   Fifth level interior granite floor pattern drawing
3   Fourth level interior granite floor pattern drawing
Following page:
    Interior of passenger ticketing and check-in area

2

passenger circulation flow. The pattern directs passengers into ticketing areas, from security pavilions down to the train platform, and from baggage claim out to ground transportation. Even though the Great Hall has relatively larger modules than those found in the ticketing, train station and baggage claim areas, all maintain a small enough scale to allow the flooring to humanize the space.

The interiors of the facility strive to satisfy the cognitive needs of the passenger terminal's patrons. Park-like seating areas with large trees are located at either end of the terminal to establish an intimate setting within such a voluminous space. In addition to the terrazo patterns in the train station, there is an arched ceiling structure pulling the passenger into the center of the space where a ring of clocks, emulating the idea of longitude, shows various times around the world. The interior design team found it necessary to create a contrast to the translucent roof within the interior space. By utilizing darker colors on the floor and walls, the patron is grounded and the roof is designed to "float" overhead.

The reason for the prevalence of stainless steel throughout the Passenger Terminal Complex is two-fold: it reinforces the technology of flight by referencing the exposed rivets, bolts and steel associated with aircraft, and it reflects the strength and durability inherent in modern aircraft design. The use of a ground swirl finish minimizes marring of the surface. Direct lighting on the stainless steel makes the finish appear to sparkle, adding an additional element of interest to the space.

Granite Flooring

A special epoxy impregnation process was incorporated to enhance the strength of the granite flooring throughout the passenger terminal. Once strengthened, the stone could then be cut as thin as nine millimeters, thereby reducing the stone flooring weight and maximizing the yield of stone from a given block.

Installation began by laying a plastic slip-sheet between the concrete flooring structure and the flooring sub-strate to avoid adhesion between the floor and the sub-strate. Since the plastic slip-sheet retards moisture evaporation on the bottom of the sub-strate, a moisture balance must be maintained with the surface of the sub-strate to avoid curling from uneven evaporation. The stone was affixed to the new sub-strate using a custom-formulated adhesive of Mapai Manufacturing's polyurethane waterproofing adhesive and fine silica sand. Secure adhesion was attained through the use of vibrators, which leveled out the adhesive to form a uniform bond with the sub-strate.

Art Program

As part of the overall program, 1% of the construction budget was allocated to fund the art program, which mandated the architects to specify areas within the design for the inclusion of artworks. A committee composed of the airport administration, project design teams and civic leaders worked with Jennifer Murphy, Art Program Administrator, to evaluate locations and recommend a shortlist of artists from submitted portfolios. The goal of this process was to enable the chosen artists to become members of the design team during the design process. The incorporation of these pieces wonderfully reflects the collaborative design process.

Opposite:
Train arrival platform with escalator of Great Hall and baggage claim
2 Art murals featured within the interiors

5

CONSTRUCTION

1

2

The construction phase is my favorite part of the architectural process. It affords the architect the excitement of seeing all the ideas and concepts coming together. (James Bradburn, Managing Principal, Fentress Bradburn Architects Ltd.)

Ground was broken on September 28, 1989, on Denver's $4.5 billion international airport situated northeast of downtown Denver on a site comprising 53 square miles, the size of Manhattan Island, or the city of San Francisco—a site greater in area than any other airport in the world. Denver International Airport is the largest contract undertaken by the City and County of Denver and was the first airport built in a major United States city since Dallas-Fort Worth, constructed in 1974. Its only other contemporary rival in terms of construction scope was the English Channel tunnel.

1&2 Pre-construction site photos

1

2

1   Grading equipment
2   International destination crossroad signage on construction site
Opposite:
    Construction cranes at approach road

1

2

1&2   Aerial photos of passenger terminal
construction

1

2

Denver International Airport opened with one passenger terminal, three concourses housing 84 gates and 40 commuter positions, 12,000 parking spaces, five runways and an office building. Expansion capabilities allow for another passenger terminal, two concourses, 374 gates, 60 commuter positions, seven additional runways, a hotel and another office building. About 110 million cubic yards of earth, one-third the amount it took to construct the Panama Canal, were moved to grade the site. An average of 2,400 workers per day for over four years, and 9,000 workers per day during peak construction, completed the building in April 1994. Due to delays associated with the installation of the first-ever automated baggage system, the airport did not open until February 28, 1995.

1   Site grading
2   Fabric roof erection

The Passenger Terminal Complex comprises two million square feet and can accommodate up to 55 million passengers per year. Fentress Bradburn Architects' flexibility throughout the construction process allowed for numerous owner and tenant changes to the passenger terminal, including the addition of over 250,000 square feet for the Destination Coded Vehicle (DCV) automated baggage-handling system after the terminal had been enclosed. This multi-modal facility, which coordinates the interaction between patrons and airplanes, cars, taxis, buses and future light rail, is made of steel from the fifth floor up, and precast and cast-in-place concrete from the fifth floor down. The fifth floor is the dividing line because the AGTS platforms and stations were constructed earlier for testing purposes.

Fentress Bradburn Architects' decision to use steel on the upper-most levels had several benefits, namely, it allowed for greater flexibility in handling the multitude of change orders caused by many of the airlines' late involvement in the process.

The Terminal Building Construction Team
The five lead contractors for the Passenger Terminal Complex at the Denver International Airport were Weitz/Cohen, PCL/Harbert, Alvarado, MA Mortenson and Hensel Phelps. Weitz/Cohen was responsible for: the grading and lime

1

2

3   4

5   6

7   8

9   10

1   Great Hall construction photo
2   Cables at south-end curtain wall
3–11 Roof construction photo series

11

1&2   Mast top construction
Below:
      Great Hall construction
  4   Fabric roof construction

1

2

4

1

2

3

5

4

1&6   South-end of passenger terminal fabric
roof section

2&3   Roof during construction

4   Roofing cable

5, 7&8   Roof during construction

6

7

8

stabilization of the earth, drilled piers and pile caps for the Passenger Terminal Complex, the AGTS platform and tunnel, floor work in the Great Hall and tenant improvements for the Airport Office Building. PCL and Harbert formed a joint venture for the construction of the Passenger Terminal Complex, the International Arrivals Building and finishes. Alvarado constructed the Airport Office Building core and shell. MA Mortenson was hired to complete the Airport Office Building's tenant improvement work, and Hensel Phelps completed the additional parking structures.

Thom Walsh and James Bradburn directed the work of on-site architects: Mike Gengler, Chris Olson, Mike Miller, Garrett Christnacht, John Gagnon and John Salisbury. Over 50 prime- and sub-consultant contracts were awarded for the design of the Passenger Terminal Complex. Eighteen prime contractors supported by over 200 subcontractors were directly associated with the construction of the entire airport.

An in-house quality assurance team, composed of architects, John Kudrycki and Joseph Solomon, conducted periodic reviews of individual progress and reviews of technological concerns at regularly scheduled team meetings. Additionally, spot checks were performed at both 35% and 75% completion levels, and at 99%, a complete review was performed.

1

2

3

4

1–4   Details of seams between section of fabric roof
5   Sequence of mast tension ring and fabric sections
6–8   Details of seams between section of fabric roof

5

6

7

8

The Construction Process

Construction began by grading the runway area and the Passenger Terminal Complex site, during which a mound was erected for the Passenger Terminal Complex to sit on. Two basins (east and west of the mound) were created to flank the complex. These basins permitted the construction of a multi-story-parking garage that allowed close-in parking, without obstructing the views of Colorado's landscape from the passenger terminal's public levels. Rough grading was performed over the entire construction site due to schedule requirements and simultaneous building. By using this approach, the building contractors became responsible for minor elevation adjustments as described in the construction documents.

Expansive soil issues necessitated additional excavation and replacement of the original soil with four feet of moisture-cured select-fill, topped with three feet of lime-stabilized select-fill. Simultaneous building on the different projects caused a lack of on-site storage; a three-mile bus ride on yet unpaved roads past a security checkpoint was required just to reach the storage site.

In August of 1991, after completion of the initial construction bid contract for the AGTS platform and stations, construction started on the landside Passenger Terminal Complex and three island-pier concourses. This contract was accelerated and made into a single contract due to the length of time needed for AGTS testing. Follow-on contractors were required to accept any preceding construction prior to starting their own work.

Airport design and construction commenced with Continental Airlines as the lone tenant. As additional airline tenants signed contracts, changes were requested to meet individual operational requirements, resulting in design changes. Two of the largest changes were the late addition of United Airlines' flow-through ticket counters and a DCV (Destination Coded Vehicle) automated baggage-handling system, a system originally envisioned to carry baggage from curbside to airplane. This system was not part of Fentress Bradburn Architect's contract; it was a design–build contract between the City of Denver and BAE Automated Systems, a Dallas-based firm that specializes in handling systems. Limited testing of the DCV prior to installation caused a major

1

1 Curbside construction

1

2

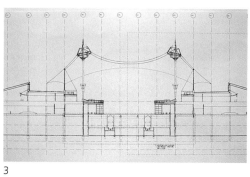

3

4

5

6

7

8

delay (over one year) and the cost overruns associated with this delay. As the construction process continued, designs to accommodate the addition of a DCV were developed, which meant installing an additional floor of approximately 250,000 square feet within the already enclosed building. These changes required two separate design teams: one developing new designs and the other identifying construction areas to be put on hold or demolished. To ensure successful system implementation and cost-effective solutions, coordination between the two teams was critical.

Constructing the Fabric Roof
The fabric roof proved to be the fastest part of the whole construction process to complete. Roof construction began in February 1992 and was completed in October 1992. The masts were erected in pairs from north to south on either side of the Great Hall, with the first steel mast rising at the northeast corner of the passenger terminal. At the bottom of each mast, top rings and covers were assembled and hoisted by winches to the top. Steel masts were stayed through the use of guy wires. Once all of the masts were in place, the fiberglass mast tops were raised and supported by a steel tension truss, which was also connected to the cable system and roof fabric. Next, the fabric panels were laid out on the temporarily carpeted Great Hall floor. The outer panels, followed by the inner panels, were then clamped to the ridge cables before being raised. Each of these panels was lifted to the fiberglass mast top. This process

1&2 Connection details of fabric roofing
   3 Graphic of roof construction process
4&5 Connection details of fabric roofing
   6 Construction site
   7 November 1992 snow storm
   8 Skylight installation
   9 Great Hall
Following page:
   Buckets line the floor for granite installation

9

1

continued along the entire length of the passenger terminal. As each panel was added, the stress to the previously tensioned units impelled the structure toward its intended shape. Meanwhile, the entire structure remained temporarily tensioned until the last panel on the south side was installed. When all of the roof units were in place, the final stressing of the structure was achieved through the downward jacking of the "octopus connection" located at each of the structure's four corners. After several go-rounds, the correct amount of pressure was achieved, creating the final shape.

During the last weekend in November of 1992, only a few months before completion, at least 12 inches of snow fell in Denver. Enough snow accumulated on the roof so that some of the modules sagged, and the valley cables had to pick up loads in the middle of the span. This proved that the addition of valley cables, identified from the wind-tunnel test results, were both necessary and viable solutions for structural stresses under certain climatic conditions.

1   Curbside construction

2   South-end curtain wall with bow trusses

Following page:
     Granite floor installation in Great Hall

2

1

2

1 Flight information display in Great Hall
2 Signage installation in the elevator lobby
Following page:
3 Cornerstone

ARCHITECTURE

1

Architecture is the manifestation of the spirit of an age, seizing upon its technical conquests. It imparts to what is to become the face of land that aspect of youth and honesty which revives the spirit, stimulates creative activity, and constitutes the new links of that unbroken chain of tradition, that chain whose link was at one time an act of creative optimism, a forward step, a constructive effort. (Le Corbusier, *Aircraft*, Universe Books, NY, 1988 [1st edn 1935], suggesting an alternative to the then-current theology practiced among architectural and engineering institutions.)

As the world becomes smaller by means of technological, political, economic and social change, design of airport facilities offers a city or a country the opportunity to portray itself to the rest of the world. These facilities have become gateways and communal showcases for those who voyage through them.

The Passenger Terminal Complex design called for a far-reaching vision coupled with imaginative building technologies. The complex is an excellent example of how materials, patterns and textures from the local environment can be strategically incorporated to address the physical, cognitive and functional needs of the user. Successfully establishing the passenger terminal as a memorable and unique symbol of the region has placed Fentress Bradburn Architects at the forefront of airport architects as a leader in the trend toward defining the airport building form in the 21st century.

2

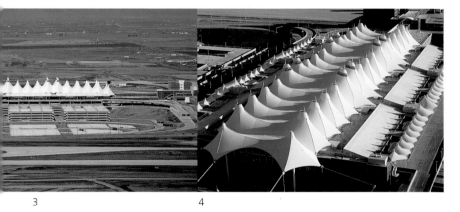

3

4

1–4
  Four different views of the Passenger Terminal
  Complex

Following page:
  Aerial view of passenger terminal with airfield
  and concourses beyond

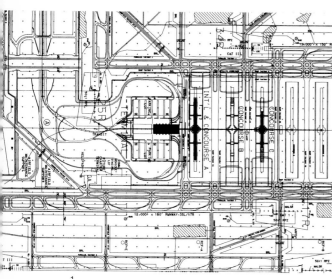

1

Fentress Bradburn Architects designed the Passenger Terminal Complex with all types of passengers in mind, including those needing special assistance. Throughout the process, Fentress Bradburn Architects conferred with the Colorado Commission for the Disabled and hence, Denver International Airport has been touted as one of the most handicapped-friendly facilities in the world. Upon arriving at the facilities, there are easily identified lanes for persons requiring assistance at tollbooth "spitter machines." The most efficient circulation paths from ground transportation to check-in to the train, as well as from the train to baggage claim to ground transportation are clearly denoted with signage. Airport personnel are continuously available to provide transportation services from parking lots to departure gates and back. Elevators were located within the secured area to aid transportation from the lower level of the Great Hall into the train station. In addition to handicapped-accessible toilets within all public restrooms, there are unisex toilets specially designed to facilitate handicapped persons and their assistants. Located throughout the complex are facilities for the deaf and hearing-impaired. Currently, the airport management is working on installing a universal public visual paging system throughout the facility.

Teflon-Coated Fiberglass Tensile-Membrane Roof
Intense design studies and critical review regarding the roof resulted in an architectural, environmental and structural solution symbolic of the Rocky Mountains. As the largest structurally integrated, Teflon-coated fiberglass tensile-membrane roof in

1   Site plan graphic
2   Passenger terminal approach road

2

1

1&Opposite:
Details of fabric roof with skylights

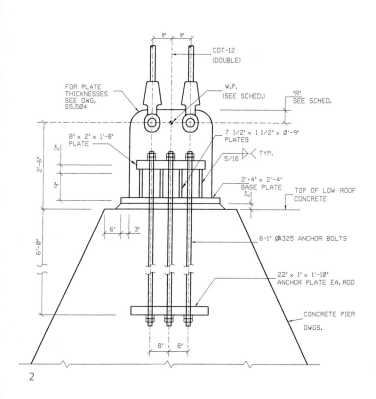

FOR PLATE
THICKNESSES
SEE DWG.
S5.504

CDT-12
(DOUBLE)

W.P.
(SEE SCHED.)

"R"
SEE SCHED.

8" × 2" × 1'-8"
PLATE

7 1/2" × 1 1/2" × 0'-9"
PLATES

5/16 TYP.

2'-4" × 2'-4"
BASE PLATE

TOP OF LOW ROOF
CONCRETE

6-1" Ø A325 ANCHOR BOLTS

22" × 1" × 1'-10"
ANCHOR PLATE EA. ROD

CONCRETE PIER
DWGS.

2

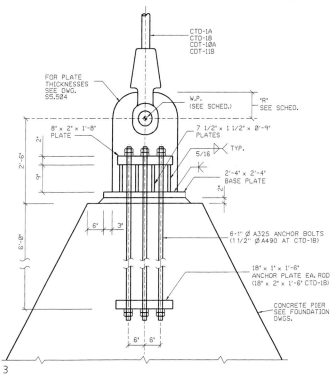

CTD-1A
CTD-1B
CDT-10A
CDT-11B

FOR PLATE
THICKNESSES
SEE DWG.
S5.504

W.P.
(SEE SCHED.)

"R"
SEE SCHED.

8" × 2" × 1'-8"
PLATE

7 1/2" × 1 1/2" × 0'-9"
PLATES

5/16 TYP.

2'-4" × 2'-4"
BASE PLATE

6-1" Ø A325 ANCHOR BOLTS
(1 1/2" Ø A490 AT CTD-1B)

18" × 1" × 1'-6"
ANCHOR PLATE EA. ROD
(18" × 2" × 1'-6" CTD-1B)

CONCRETE PIER
SEE FOUNDATION
DWGS.

3

4

5

Opposite & 2–5
Details of tie-down connections

1

the world, it satisfies an imaginative aesthetic vision coupled with unique, cost-effective building technologies and economical energy systems.

The tensile-membrane roof is anchored in place through a cable system more than 10 miles long and using 30,000 clamps. A multi-functional steel mast, wrapped in a fiberglass shroud, braces each of the 34 peaks. Features housed at the steel masts include a lift basket for maintenance crews to reach hose bibs that clean the exterior roof, and platforms containing up-lights and speakers for the public address system.

Natural Light

Research studies show sunlight is associated with positive mood and altruistic behavior. When the indoor environment is pleasant, people are more comfortable and have more positive interactions with each other. Denver International Airport's terminal is a great example of how a space can be responsive to people's desire for natural light. (Dr. Diane Martichuski, Professor of Psychology, University of Colorado, Boulder).

1 View of curbside with curbside canopies

Skylights are incorporated in the caps of the eight tallest peaks, adding natural light to the diffused light coming through the Teflon-coated fiberglass roof. Skepticism surrounded the issue of installing skylights, not only because of maintenance concerns, but also because there were no skylights in Denver's airport history. However, Fentress Bradburn Architects supported their necessity based on the need to add warmth, animate the interior space and cast shadows as elements in creating the illusion of outdoor spaces within the terminal itself. Collaboration between the proponents and opponents over the skylight issue resulted in a strategic reduction in the number of skylights from the total specified in the initial

design. Together, fabric roofing and skylights provide enough natural light, both direct and diffused, to sustain plant life. This has eliminated the need for artificial lighting in the ticketing and check-in area and the Great Hall during daylight hours.

Passenger Terminal

Mountainous shapes and textures have been incorporated in the roof structure, the curbside canopies, granite floor patterns and select wall panels. Dwayne Nuzum, University of Colorado's School of Architecture and Planning Dean in 1993, recognized the roof structure as an element capable of classifying Denver International Airport

1

2

1   View of Airport Office Building from Great Hall

2   Interior view of fabric roof masts with crows-nest

Following page:
   North-end of Great Hall with Jeppesen statue,
   for whom the passenger terminal was named

as a peer of both Eero Saarinen's TWA (Trans World Airlines) terminals at Kennedy International Airport and Dulles International Airport.

The passenger terminal space's tranquil nature is inextricably tied to the interiors. A clearly contextual and patron-oriented approach is evident in the warm, rich undertones of the granite, carpeting and furniture. Subliminal floor patterns lead patrons naturally from point-to-point, helping to ease the anxiety and stress often associated with travel. The scale of interior details helps to minimize the space's expanse (150 feet across the lower level and 210 feet across at the upper level), making it appear smaller and more intimate.

> Elevator core areas will be faced with Colorado yule marble, beautiful white stone that adds to the feeling of natural light. And in the train platforms and stairways, layered red sandstone 'mountains' are topped with marble sheets. If the designers wanted this place to 'look like Colorado', they truly succeeded here. (Mary Voelz Chandler, Art and Architecture Critic, "Airport's Tent Roof, Lightly Stand Out, But Questions Remain", *The Rocky Mountain News*, June 6, 1993, p. 39A)

Great Hall

The unencumbered volume of space of the Great Hall together with vast amounts of natural light readily allow users to relax, shop, eat and conduct business. By utilizing a raised roof, as opposed to the flat roofs of Atlanta, Dallas or Newark, much of the typical oppression associated with large airport structures is alleviated.

While travelers are typically en route to the train upon leaving the ticketing and curbside area, the Great Hall space causes them to slow down because there is something to see — a moment to experience. Unlike airports of the more recent past, the design ensures passengers, employees and patrons do not feel "processed." Recognizing that travel can be stressful enough, the Great Hall conveys an interest in the well-being of passengers by making the transitory time more calm and enjoyable. The luminous freestanding south-end curtain wall provides views of the Colorado landscape.

Opposite:
    Interior view of the Great Hall from the north-end of the airport
Following page:
    Interior view of south-end curtain wall

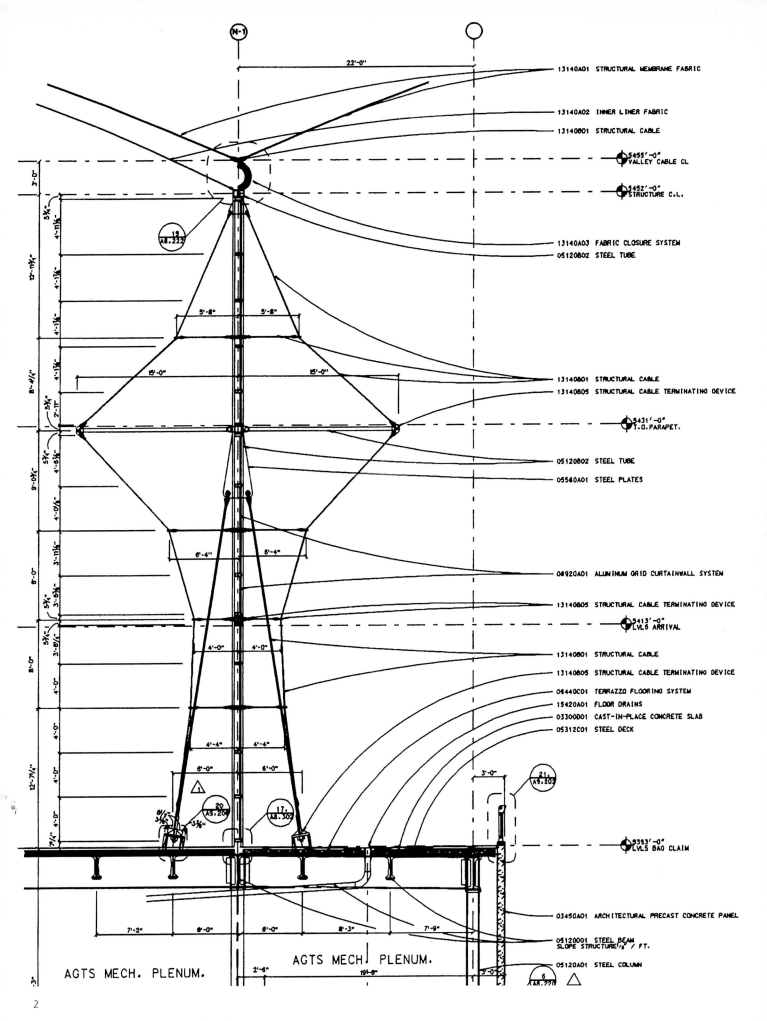

13140A01 STRUCTURAL MEMBRANE FABRIC

13140A02 INNER LINER FABRIC

13140B01 STRUCTURAL CABLE

⊕ 5455'-0"
VALLEY CABLE CL

⊕ 5452'-0"
STRUCTURE C.L.

13140A03 FABRIC CLOSURE SYSTEM
05120B02 STEEL TUBE

13140B01 STRUCTURAL CABLE
13140B05 STRUCTURAL CABLE TERMINATING DEVICE

⊕ 5431'-0"
T.O.PARAPET.

05120B02 STEEL TUBE

05560A01 STEEL PLATES

08920A01 ALUMINUM GRID CURTAINWALL SYSTEM

13140B05 STRUCTURAL CABLE TERMINATING DEVICE

⊕ 5413'-0"
LVL6 ARRIVAL

13140B01 STRUCTURAL CABLE

13140B05 STRUCTURAL CABLE TERMINATING DEVICE
09440C01 TERRAZZO FLOORING SYSTEM
15420A01 FLOOR DRAINS
03300D01 CAST-IN-PLACE CONCRETE SLAB
05312C01 STEEL DECK

⊕ 5393'-0"
LVL5 BAG CLAIM

03450A01 ARCHITECTURAL PRECAST CONCRETE PANEL

05120D01 STEEL BEAM
SLOPE STRUCTURE⅛"/FT.

05120A01 STEEL COLUMN

AGTS MECH. PLENUM.

AGTS MECH. PLENUM.

2

Opposite:
Exterior view of south-end curtain wall

2   Detailed graphic of south-end curtain wall bow trusses

1

1   Signage with escalator to baggage claim
2   View from interior bridge of flight-information displays and security check-points

Following pages:

3   Train departure platform with clocks featuring times from around the world
4   Lighting fixture detail in Great Hall

It is not until people enter the picture that scale becomes evident and the sheer size of the space is realized. Security pavilions, art exhibits, museum displays, information booths, seating areas, telephones, ATMs, multi-user flight information displays (MUFIDs) and carpet help make the lower level more intimate. Fentress Bradburn Architects recommended that upper level bridges be accepted as design modifications because it was realized that the user would be able to cross the space without engaging the persons on the lower level. Additionally, parking on either side of the terminal regardless of the traveler's initial destination at the airport, would be encouraged.

Storefronts relate to the south-end curtain wall through the utilization of clear glass, which also increases the displayable area and opens the space, giving patrons easier access. Each day, over 60,000

2

passengers pass by the storefronts lining both the upper and lower level perimeters as they move from ticketing and drop-off to security. Signage, strategically denoted with both parallel and perpendicular blade signs to the entrance, enables all patrons to clearly identify the merchant.

Granite floor patterns direct passengers from both security pavilions (centrally located on the lower level of the Great Hall) down an escalator and into a conjoining platform area. The AGTS runs to all three concourses every two minutes during the day, and then decreases to every five minutes in the late evening. Upon arrival in the main terminal from the AGTS, passengers are greeted with a wall of MUFIDs (Multi-user Flight Information Displays) embedded in red sandstone.

Dual Curbside and Ticketing

In essence, the terminal is folded back on itself, allowing 5,400 feet of curbside and 1,800 feet of ticketing counter space to be consolidated into a 900-foot-long building that requires only one train station, as opposed to the two that would be required for an 1,800-foot-long terminal. More importantly, the distance that a passenger is required to traverse is reduced. Dual curbside access is separated into three levels, easing the congestion of public and private vehicles commonly experienced at most major airports, and allowing for a greater number of close-in parking spaces. This configuration also allows the parking structures to be discreetly tucked into the basins flanking either side of the building, so that unobstructed views of the Colorado landscape are available from the drop-off level on both sides of the terminal.

SAO PAULO NEW YORK MEXICO C

PARIS MUNICH ROME HONG KONG TOKYO

Do Not Enter

3

4

1

1   Baggage claim carousel

Baggage Claim

The baggage claim areas are located directly below the ticketing counters on both sides of the terminal. Due to the addition of the mezzanine level between levels four and five during construction, the ceiling height was reduced by approximately six feet. Coffered ceiling tile with indirect lights provide a more open feeling in this space.

Walkways within the baggage area are clearly denoted by granite tile patterns that are designed to lead the patron out to the curbside areas where taxis, buses and other transportation vehicles are available. The area immediately surrounding the carousels is carpeted to reduce noise and provide a less rigid surface for standing patrons.

1

2

1   Clerestories and fabric roof detailing
2   Uplighting of fabric roof at night

Airport Office Building

The airport administration offices are housed in a building that is a complementary backdrop to the passenger terminal. The administration chose a less prominent façade in accordance with the more utilitarian goal of promoting the airport as a whole, and the passenger terminal in particular. Given this less prominent façade, the use of similar base materials was intended to maintain the architectural focus on the passenger terminal.

The master plan called for two identical 125,000-square-foot buildings on either side of the bridge to the International Arrivals Building. The office building to the west was constructed in conjunction with the terminal building, and the office building to the east is to be constructed in the future. The purpose behind this configuration is to maintain the line of symmetry while permitting 250,000 square feet of office space within the Federal Aviation Administration height restriction guidelines.

1

2

3

1 Panoramic view of the Airport Office Building to the passenger terminal
2 Airport Office Building extending from the terminal
3 International Arrivals Bridge from passenger terminal to Airport Office Building
Following page:
    View of south-end at dusk

7
GOALS AND
ACCOMPLISHMENTS

1

Denver International Airport was planned for not only our children, but our children's children. (Hana Rocek, Manager of Design, City and County of Denver)

The airport creators' progressive vision set a future-oriented precedent for this facility and the Rocky Mountain region. Denver International Airport has encouraged capital investment in the region, in part by making the area more easily accessible. In 1997, *The Denver Post* announced that the airport had thus far spawned over $1.3 billion in airport-related construction.

Since 1990, the United States has had a very strong and growing economy, yet Colorado in particular stands out as a success story. Statistics released by Western Blue Chip Economic Forecasts clearly illustrate increases in current personal income, real personal income, wage and salary employment, retail sales, manufacturing employment, population and a falling unemployment rate. Both current and real personal incomes have risen by 180% from 1990 to 1998. Wage and salary employment has increased by 135% and manufacturing employment experienced an increase of 107% while the unemployment rate decreased by 67%. Retail sales have increased by 175% while the population growth rate only increased by 120% (Western Blue Chip Economic Forecast January/February 1994 – 1998: May 1999; 1998 Current US Dollars of Personal Income [millions] consensus; and 1998 Real Personal Income [millions] estimate). Colorado remains one of the nation's most economically stable states, and is predicted to have an auspicious future.

The 1996 FAA figures of the nation's 20 most active airports show Denver International Airport with the lowest percentage of delays in the country at 0.19%. Furthermore, in 1997, it was ranked as the seventh busiest airport in the United States with 32.3 million passengers.

While the airport has yet to reach full capacity, growth estimates are being far exceeded. For example, in 1999, concessions at the airport operated at 90% above estimates. In fact, in March 1997, the airport was able to lower landing fees by 16% because rent income was so high. Soon, all of the airport's counters will be fully utilized due to United Airlines' aggressive "hubbing" operation. Also involved in United Airlines' expansion is its intention to increase the number of gates in order to accommodate expanded service.

Several projects are scheduled to begin construction, including an additional parking garage, a terminal hotel and paving the sixth runway. Light rail continues to sit on the horizon as local public transportation officials address financial issues. Whether light rail or the next terminal module expansion occurs first, the right-of-way has been reserved for the implementation of a light rail connection to the city.

From somebody who spends their life on an airplane – I continually hear people all around the world complimenting it. (Tucker Hart Adams, a prominent Denver economist and president of Adams Group, Inc.)

1   Interior view looking south

AFTERWORD

Emerging Trends in Airport Architecture
by Curtis Fentress

Since designing Denver International Airport's Passenger Terminal Complex, Fentress Bradburn Architects has had the opportunity to work on numerous airport facilities. Our knowledge and experience with international airport architecture continues to grow, establishing our firm as an artistically and technologically innovative leader among our competitors.

While each new terminal design adheres to our long-standing design philosophy of merging contextual regionalism and user specificity in the creation of an architecturally significant landmark, each design is as unique to the location as it is to the client. Yet, as we enter the new millenium, there are strong indications of what airport architecture must encompass in the future. The needs of the passenger are becoming more and more important as annual enplanement numbers continue to rise. Even today, passengers have a choice among a variety of origins, destinations and connection airports to utilize. As airports become larger components in local and national economies, the creation of an inviting and convenient environment for users is essential to an airport's success.

The ever-increasing diversity among traveler demographics is forcing airports to broaden passenger services, which will not only enhance the experience of patrons, but also help airports to take full advantage of this lucrative market. Airports contain some of the most desirable clientele, persons with ample time and discretionary funds. Often these individuals have time to purchase gifts, connect to the Internet, take conference calls, eat foods of their choice or simply relax. By improving services and convenience to meet these needs, airports will be building and expanding on the already successful trend of branding, local theming and street pricing.

At Fentress Bradburn Architects, we are continuing to design airport terminals with these issues in mind. In fact, some airports have incorporated such conveniences as post offices, hair salons and fitness centers. Conference areas and other business centers allow business travelers to conduct meetings within the confines of the airport. Further, smokers' bars and lounges are provided within otherwise smoke-free environments. Many of these lounges incorporate isolated venting technologies.

We are sitting on the cusp of a movement toward implementing additional "extras," such as Denver and Burbank International Airports' valet services, which return cars washed, tuned and detailed. Expanded customer service options are endless: for example, catalogue ordering to augment concessionaires' currently available merchandise will soon be available. Some shops may even offer travelers the ability to pick up purchases at the arrival gate.

The following airports provide great examples of how our firm implements its growing experience on each individual project: Inchon International Airport in the Republic of South Korea; Second Bangkok International Airport Terminal in Thailand; Doha International Airport in Qatar; New Terminal Area for Madrid-Barajas Airport in Spain; Central Terminal redevelopment and expansion at Seattle-Tacoma International Airport in Washington; Reina Sofia Airport in Tenerife-Sur; Terminal Complex expansion at Vienna Airport in Austria; and Munich International Airport's Terminal Two in Germany.

1

1   Rendering of passenger terminal from approach road

Inchon International Airport

In association with Korean architectural firms Baum, Hi-Lim, Jung-Lim and Wodushi Architects, we won the international design competition for the $1.1 billion Main Terminal Building at the New Inchon International Airport in a unanimous (11-0) jury decision. The jury endorsed our design because it "fully understands this new world-class hub airport will be the gateway to Korea of the new age. The design team's efforts to draw harmony between Korean images and global design trends and technologies are outstanding."

The site is located on a man-made landfill connecting two islands in the Yellow Sea, 50 kilometers west of Seoul's city center. It is within three-and-one-half hours flying time of 40 cities, each with a population of more than one million people, making it an ideal location for a regional hub. The Main Terminal Building covers 5,935,000 square feet (550,000 square meters) distributed over six levels. Scheduled to open in January 2001, the terminal will have 46 connected wide-body gates.

1

1   Aerial view of construction site
2   Aerial view of passenger terminal
3   Aerial view of passenger terminal model
4   Aerial view of passenger terminal roof

2

3

4

1

2

Our vision for Inchon International Airport was to create a treasured national landmark that embodies the art, tradition and culture of the Korean peninsula. Although Korea is an ancient land, rich in history, it has also become a very modern country and actively participates in the global market. While the design is reflective of ancient Korean culture in its forms and use of materials and colors, it also reflects the advanced technologies of contemporary Korea in overall image and use of sophisticated building materials.

This inspirational imagery used in the building is seen in clearly defined structural systems, such as long colonnades of round columns. These structures add rhythm and pattern to the space, reminiscent of the alternating square and round columns of ancient Korean palaces that pay homage to a harmony between heaven and earth. The imagery used at the airport continues in pattern and color as applied to structural members, walls, floors and ceilings, which depict traditional stories and underscore the building's function. The sweep of the airport roofline transmits the story of thousands of years of traditional Korean architecture. Processional arrangements in the layout also delineate function and societal hierarchies.

Inchon International Airport is also flooded with cultural images denoting the local geography. The cultural use of color gives identity to certain hues as being distinctly Korean. Colorful costumes, traditional dress and bold signage demonstrate the importance of red, blue and yellow as accent colors for cultural images, which are as influential today as they were centuries ago. These colors used in conjunction with the muted earth colors of gold, green and blue create a powerful palette that appears timeless. Soft white and gray hues on walls and ceiling planes provide a neutral background to complement the brightness of the city nearby.

Koreans use patterns to describe visual images, tell stories and add visual interest to their architecture. We have also used such patterns, like the symbols for earth and sky, to mark intersections and define functions and zones. The terminal design also applies these patterns to its landside (earth) and airside (sky) aspects.

3

4

5

Linear graphics found in the floor pattern directionally cue passengers through the airport, just as strong linear elements in local palace roof structures helped direct the movement of royal processions. These lines visually direct passengers to ticketing, security, customs and immigration.

A pattern created by the division of screens and windows on ancient Korean palaces is the inspiration for the terminal's wall-panel system. The circle, part of the national symbol on the Korean flag, symbolizes the sun and moon, and represents the harmony between heaven and earth. In the airport, the circle is used as a contrast to the linear patterns and identifies specific points in circulation zones.

It was important that the terminal and concourses would make Inchon International Airport as enjoyable and comfortable as possible for travelers. We have humanized the spaces within the high-tech atmosphere of a large international airport by creating an environment that is inviting and user-friendly through the use of warm colors, spatial layouts and lighting. Location of spaces such as restrooms, gate entrances and retail outlets are reinforced by consistency of design and finish material, helping the passenger easily comprehend

the building and navigate through various zones. This inviting environment is further enhanced through comfortable seating areas, convenient amenities and easily accessed retail spaces.

International air traveler's first and last images of a country are those created at the port of entry or exit. As a symbol of confidence in the commercial future of the Republic of South Korea and Southeast Asia, Inchon International Airport's dramatic architecture also reflects Korea's cultural heritage and its technological, economic and social achievements.

1   Concourse roof construction
2   Great Hall and concourse roof trusses
3   Construction view of Great Hall
4&5   Rendering of passenger ticketing and
      check-in areas

Second Bangkok International Airport Terminal
Presented with the task of creating a comprehensive airport facility for Thailand's Second Bangkok International Airport, our firm designed an architectural complex that is expressive of the excitement of travel and the spirit of the Thai people. This airport was designed to function as the new global aviation gateway for Southeast Asia, Thailand and the world.

The Passenger Terminal Complex competition required a highly efficient world-class design of a hub airport that accommodates both origin–destination and transfer traffic. In our submission, the challenge was to explore alternative configurations to become more familiar with programmatic issues that would lead to the final design. Sixteen alternatives were developed and evaluated based on passenger convenience, airport operation, aesthetics and economy of cost and construction. The final design provided an integrated passenger terminal complex, including passenger terminal building, elevated frontage roads serving landside vehicular traffic at the terminal, a vehicular parking structure adjacent to the passenger terminal, integrated offices, operations support facilities, future rail access to the passenger terminal and landscaping.

Five topographical regions constitute Thailand and are reflected in our design: fertile central plains; a mountainous northern region; a semi-arid plateau in the northeast; a narrow isthmus in the south with hilly rain forests; and a coastline of bays and coves with numerous outlying islands. In addition, four components of life in the Buddhist tradition include functions of the natural environment as it relates to the human body: earth to body, water to blood, wind to breath and fire to emotion. All four images of the natural environment are integrated into the design through the use of materials, patterns and textures as they relate to the functional and aesthetic requirements of the building.

Currents and patterns of wind and water are also frequently used as symbols of flight, as is the movement of cloud formations across the sky and waves across the surface of the sea. The design incorporates these metaphors in its larger spaces, broad vistas and aerodynamic structures. For example, kites and canopies representing flight impart a feeling of lightness and movement

1

1

2

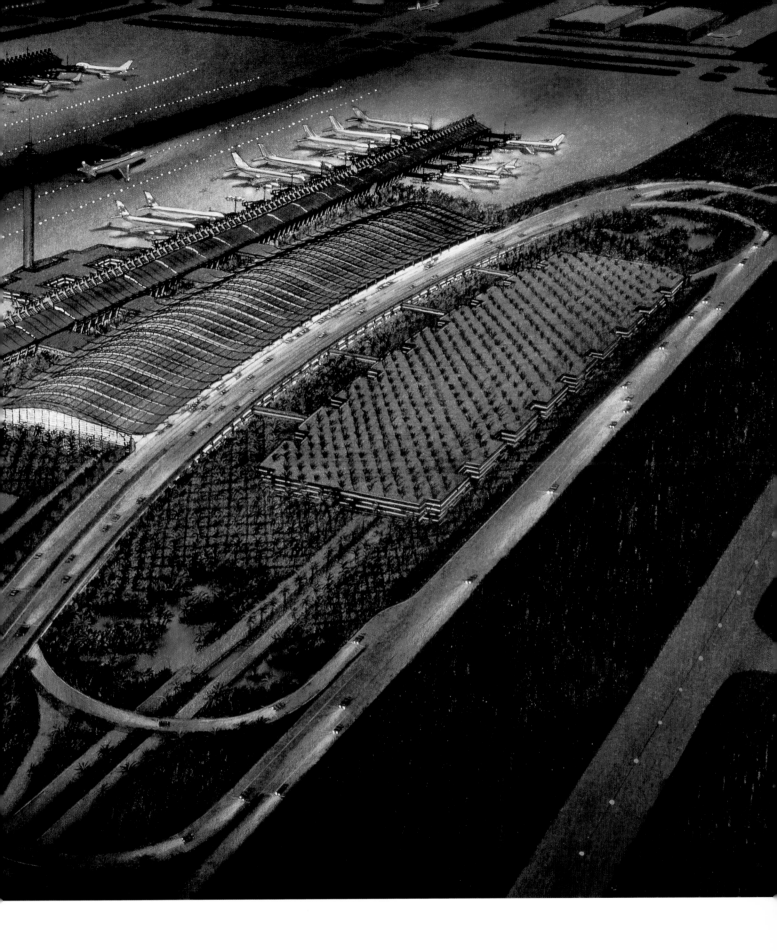

1 Rendering of aerial view
2 Model of aerial view

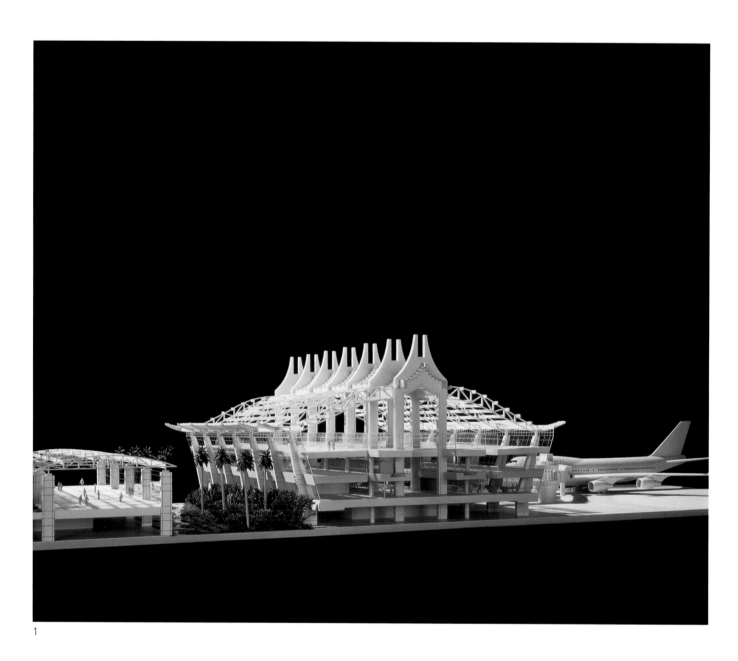

1

throughout the terminal complex to animate spaces and invoke a heightened level of excitement once associated with the travel experience.

The design also provides world-class innovative and technical facilities in the areas of phased expansion, passenger convenience and airport operations. Fentress Bradburn Architect's design concept and philosophy reflect the ancient and modern cultures of Thailand and the native landscape, as well as the spirituality and philosophies of Thailand's people. We found inspiration in the many shapes and forms of the surrounding natural and man-made environments. Like *khlongs* (the canals of Bangkok), the form of

the runways, taxiways and concourses are planned in a linear progression of movement. This straight path of travel greatly enhances passengers' ease of movement through the passenger terminal building. Further, as the spine of the concourse opens up through a series of skylights, the atria spaces close down like a canopy of lush vegetation along the banks of these canals.

From exterior to interior, the Second Bangkok International Airport structure comes alive with tradition and symbolism. Approaching roads and surrounding land are densely planted with grasses, shrubs, trees and lush flower gardens, rich and magnificent in color. The landscape makes

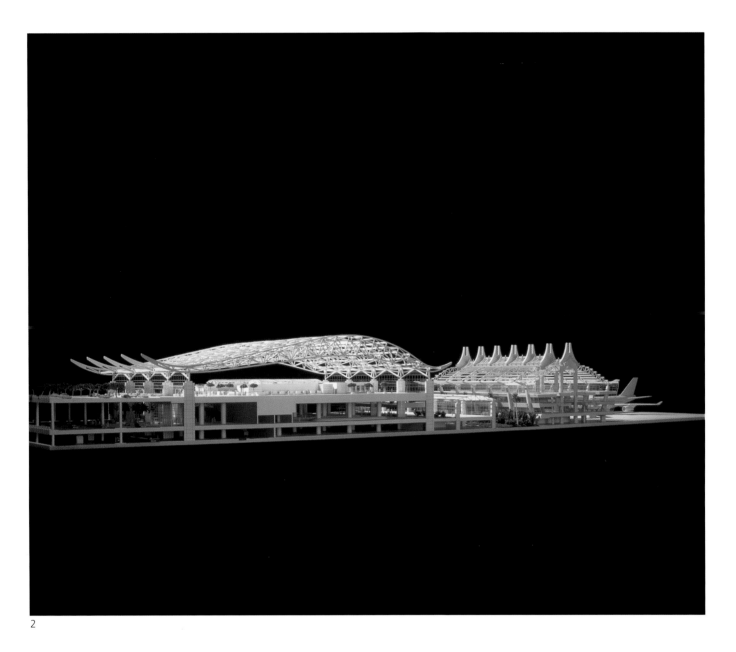

2

transitions from groves to hardwood forest, symbolizing the forests of northern Thailand. At the final approach, draping bougainvillea and flowering vines are layered along the terraced walls, while palms and bamboo arch outward from the terraces to create a floral portal that signifies the arrival to the terminal.

Within the facility, the design explores and captures the wonder and excitement of flight, using innovative design technology coupled with traditional and native materials. Borrowing familiar images, the roof structure is reminiscent of the sinuous shape of a *nan* boat or royal barge, while the lotus flower of Thailand is referenced in the concourse ceiling.

Throughout the facility, natural daylighting and interior landscaping have been incorporated to provide a pleasant travel experience for all passengers. Skylights allow large amounts of direct daylight to energize the space. In these areas, lush greenery and landscaping impart a feeling of the outdoors, reducing the need for artificial illumination and, therefore, energy costs.

Within the "meeters and greeters" hall located at the front of the landside terminal, an abundance of natural materials, landscaping and traditional Thai colors are designed to mitigate jet lag. The selection of finish materials was carefully considered for functional requirements, durability and maintenance. In keeping with the design

1

concept, materials were selected for pattern, rich color and texture. From the cast-in-place and precast concrete, colored in an earthy, warm tone for the exterior of the terminal, to the pattern and color of the granite and carpet-tile floor patterns of the interior, the finishes and materials selected reinforce continuity throughout the airport.

We continually focus on passenger comfort and convenience. All elements of the passenger terminal building design provide simple, easy orientation and convenient circulation for passengers. The linear concourse minimizes passenger connect times from the furthest gate while also allowing for the installation of an above-grade automated people-mover system at any phase during development.

Although no longer the royal residence, Thailand's Grand Palace serves as a great historical symbol. While used only on special State occasions, it remains the symbolic heart of the capital. The architectural styles of the Grand Palace and the shrine of Wat Phra Keo vary from pure Thai to Victorian and Italian Renaissance. Together, they offer exquisite decorative, mythological and spiritual images, which served as a great source of architectural inspiration to the design of this airport.

Thailand's Second Bangkok International Airport was designed with maximum flexibility of efficient operation to accommodate long-term development. This elegant, unique and culturally appropriate solution could impact terminal design for years to come.

1   Rendering of "meeters and greeters" hall
Opposite:
      Rendering of concourse interiors

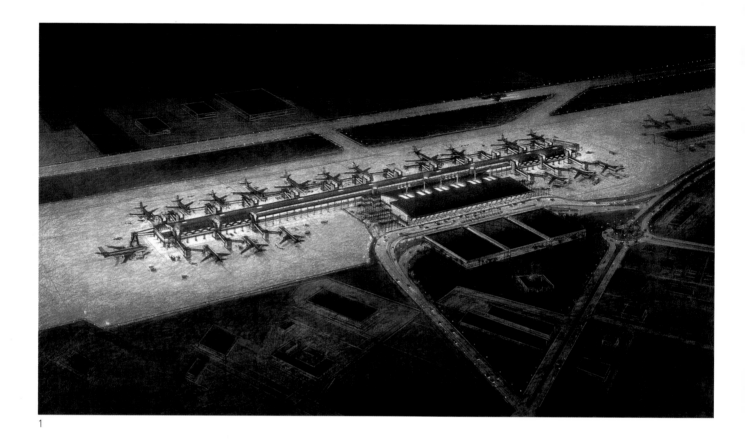

1

Doha International Airport

Fentress Bradburn Architects also won the international design competition for the Doha International Airport in Qatar, commissioned by the Qatari Ministry of Municipal Affairs and Agriculture. To be completed in 2002, it is located west of an existing runway and adjacent to existing terminals, which remained fully functional and operational during the construction of the new facility.

The terminal is composed of three levels. All facilities for international arrival passengers are located in arrivals processing on the first level, including immigration, security checkpoints, baggage claim, customs facilities, "meeters and greeters" hall and various support facilities. The second level is the arrivals concourse leading to the arrivals processing area, a transfer-passenger processing checkpoint and an airport hotel for use by "extended stay" transfer passengers. Contained on the third level are all facilities for departing-passenger processing functions, including the departures hall, security checkpoints, passenger check-in, outbound customs and emigration, retail and concessions.

Addressing both context and region, the design of Doha International Airport utilizes cultural and religious symbols drawn from Islam and the local Qatari *dhows* (traditional fishing craft) to create an image that is at once recognizable and new. The terminal design leaves a dramatic, lasting impression on both its international audience and Qatari travelers. Qatar's enhanced aviation facilities positively influence the image that international business people and tourists have of the nation. Its landmark architecture is reflective of Qatar's cultural, economic and social heritage and achievements. The Doha International Airport is regarded as a symbol of confidence in the future of Qatar and the Middle East.

The terminal facility is clearly inspired by traditional Qatari architectural elements. The ticketing hall roof springs from central supporting masts, whose arching form recalls the form of Qatari *dhows*. Airside gate towers mimic local wind towers, while the curving forms of the massive windswept sand dunes surrounding Qatar's coastline provide inspiration for the curves of the terminal complex roof. Further, richly detailed patterns used on floors, walls and exterior glass are influenced by

3

2

4

traditional Qatari patterns, such as the rich tapestry on display at the Qatar National Museum.

Exterior palette materials include cast-in-place and precast white and earthy sand-color concrete, which recalls typical local building coloration, as well as the sandy coastline of Qatar. Complimented with a traditional Qatari-patterned ceramic frit, the exterior glass not only creates an underlying sense of place, but also aids in reducing heat gain. Due to the harsh nature of the desert sun, all skylight glazing was also finished with a cloud-patterned ceramic frit.

The overall design of Doha International Airport optimizes passenger comfort and convenience in a variety of ways. The terminal and concourse are configured to clarify and simplify passenger flows and aircraft operations. Passengers may also find refuge in rotunda-shaped duty-free zones, which recall the turreted corners of nearby aging military forts. In short, our comprehensive design has a gentle, soaring quality, expressing flight, rhythm, movement and direction.

1　Rendering of curbside entrance to the terminal

1

2

3

1   Rendering of concourse interiors
2   Rendering of retail areas
3   New control tower

New Terminal Area for Madrid-Barajas Airport

The play of light at Madrid's latitude and the architectural traditions of the western Mediterranean served to organize our design submission on the New Terminal Area at Madrid-Barajas International Airport. While elements of Spanish architecture evoke a sense of history and place particular to Madrid, the design's integrated tensile fabric roof diffuses light to the interior, creating an airy look and feel. From the outside, the structure has the white, opaque look of a Mediterranean building; inside, the effect is luminous as light penetrates the fabric and plays off the supporting latticework. An occasional clerestory brings in direct natural light, creating an interplay of light and shadow, also characteristic of Spanish architecture.

Arches, vaults, columns and interior patios, all essential expressions of Spanish architecture, fulfill both the need for a historically evocative motif, while also serving as a system of structural elements to bridge wide spans and cover the extensive area of the Great Hall space. Meanwhile, ceiling vaults reference grand civic spaces within the terminal.

Other traditional building elements like shades, cloisters, loggias, galleries, pergolas and screens, provide shelter and help to organize and humanize the space. Further, the grid of arches and columns in the main hall is suggestive of the region's Islamic influences. This hierarchy of arches symbolic of a gateway harkens back to ancient Roman architecture.

From ocher to burnt sienna, arrays of colors characterize Madrid's arid plain, while the Jarama and Henares rivers carve green paths through this geography. Our design responded to this context by creating an organic structure, rising in a gentle sequence of waves, using hues from the earthy palette of the local region.

Transparency as a design motivator necessitated the intensive use of glass, which was interspersed with cork, carpet and fabric-coated walls, internal partitions and panels. Shadows best display the colored tiles and decorative ceramics that are characteristic of Spanish architectural heritage, and act as the main counterpoint to the decorative materials used.

Regular geometrical arrangements permit the repetition of elements and aid circulation flows, while at the same time reducing fabrication time and cost. The floor is composed of native granite slabs, highly resistant to wear and easy to clean. These are alternated with carpeted rest areas, all arranged in keeping with traditional tones and geometrical patterns. Rich in historical and contextual references, and executed with a humanistic touch, the design of the New Terminal Area for Madrid-Barajas International Airport is both timeless and memorable.

1   Aerial view of concourse terminal model

1

2

3

4

1   Rendering of Ticketing Hall
2   Rendering of Great Hall
3   Rendering of passenger terminal
4   Aerial view of concourse and terminal model

Munich International Airport's Terminal Two

The international design competition among 15 invited architectural firms for Munich International Airport's Terminal Two in Germany called for an environmentally aware design, in harmony with the pre-existing Munich Airport Center. The goal was to establish circulation flows, while providing the highest level of passenger comfort and convenience, all in a transparent, voluminous, open structure.

The program for Terminal Two included a new landside terminal facility, domestic and international concourses and structured parking facilities. Also included were associated roadways and elevated curbside roadway structures to access the terminal and parking facilities, the existing hotel and the Munich Airport Center. Additionally, the area was master-planned for a future hotel facility and an office complex.

Our design submission was an elaboration on the criteria mentioned in an innovative and artistic manner. Our transparent, voluminous, open design is achieved through a systematic arrangement of ceiling apertures and glass façades. This arrangement establishes a relationship between the exterior and interior, and creates a bright and friendly environment. The design is of a simple, easily understood airport terminal that provides services as conveniently as possible.

Retail facilities are continuous along passenger routes so travelers can shop, eat and drink, or take advantage of any of the other numerous services this facility offers without ever having to venture off the route to their respective gates. The central Great Hall organizes the landside terminal portion of the facility, offering passengers and visitors a unique and interesting spatial experience.

The design of Terminal Two stands in harmony with the Munich Airport Center's Terminal One and the remaining Munich International Airport buildings, despite the unique architecture of each of these facilities. Terminal Two is just as unique, yet works toward the creation of a wholly complimentary campus. In keeping with the underlying design philosophy, the sweeping curve of Terminal Two's roof meets gracefully with the soaring space of Munich Airport Center's forum, while also providing for the greatest possible freedom in future developments. The interaction of these two spaces is respectful without being competitive, and Munich Airport Center still remains the center of the airport complex's internal organization.

Terminal Two is designed as a centrally organized terminal with an attached linear concourse. Planned to accommodate hubbing operations, the terminal provides clear, simple passenger

1

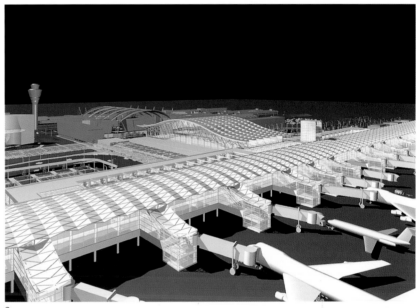

2

3

1–3   Renderings of terminal, concourse and
        approach road
Opposite:
        Aerial view of airport complex

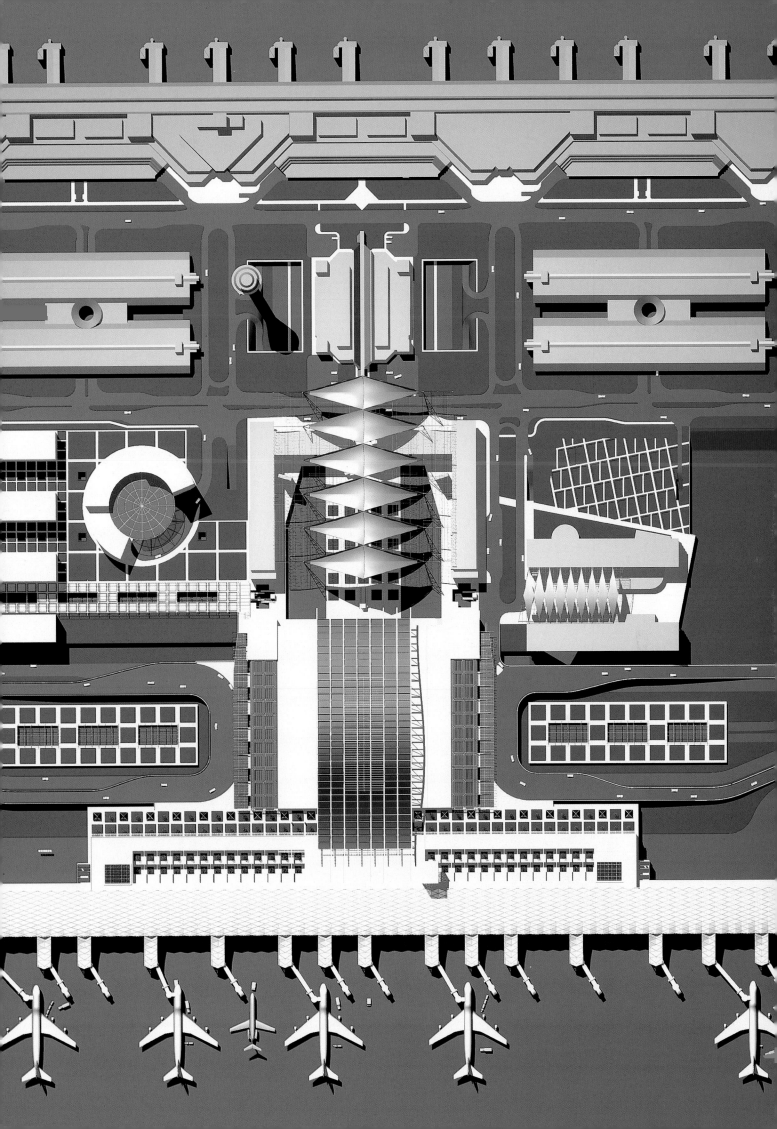

1   Site plan graphic
Opposite:
    Aerial view of model

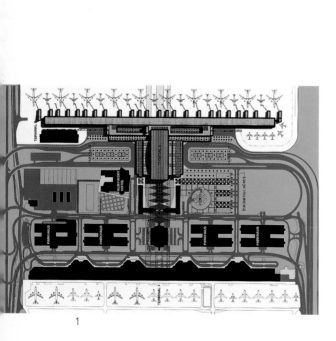

1

circulation. The continuation of the logical circulation system allows passengers to easily orient themselves within the complex. Passengers are offered a direct enclosed connection from Terminal One to Terminal Two. Landscaping and axial hierarchy are linked to form one continuous area. Exterior walkways tie Munich Airport Center and Terminal Two together, both functionally and aesthetically. The layout of Terminal Two continues and completes the axial circulation relationships established by Terminal One, the central area and Munich Airport Center. Throughout the facility, passengers quickly gain a firm understanding of the relationship between each of the buildings, which is important, given the expansive distances between each building.

Direct natural daylighting is incorporated into all public areas at all levels of the building. The north and south clerestory walls of the Great Hall are orientated to focus the front door image outward. Along with daylighting, extensive garden areas are designed to soften the hard edges of the building and its perceived mass. To keep all users of the facility in touch with nature, interior gardens are placed in both public areas and office spaces.

Our design is economical both in construction and long-term operating costs. For example, the Great Hall roof structure is unique in form but simple in construction. Furthermore, simplicity of the concourse layout will allow construction of repetitive spans and systems. Natural daylighting and ventilation will also aid in the reduction of energy costs.

Clear phasing scenarios, offering logical, simple expansion of the facility, will aid the airport in future growth development. Attractive and appropriately located airport concessions will also make a significant difference in passenger enjoyment and airport revenue. The opaque exterior appearance is a constant for the campus and a prevalent German architectural characteristic.

At Fentress Bradburn Architects, we continue to study these and other trends as we design today for tomorrow's spaces. Our goal is not only to maintain an awareness of what works now, but also to create spaces that anticipate future needs. With each new project, we have the opportunity to create landmark, archetypal, innovative space.

1

2

1&2   Rendering of Great Hall space

Terminal Complex Expansion at Vienna Airport

The international design competition for the Terminal Complex expansion at Vienna Airport in Austria was by invitation-only, involving 16 internationally acclaimed architects. Our entry finished among the top five. The competition was in two parts: a design concept competition for the expansion of the existing Vienna International Airport, and a city planning concept competition for future airport growth, with the underlying goal of creating a landmark image for Vienna and Austria.

Design and functional challenges arose due to the site location, which was defined by three major physical attributes: the existing airport was contained between two currently operational runways; the autobahn defined the northwestern edge of the site; and existing buildings were located adjacent to the existing airport terminal. Expansion of the airport involved adding 24 new gates and doubling the terminal's current check-in, ticketing and baggage facilities. Our design, an elongated structure that reaches out into the landscape, provided architectural and functional continuity among the other facilities at the site.

Our design is supported by *piolitis*, columns that allow landscape and traffic to flow beneath the structure. Housed within this building are six levels that function as corridors connecting the parking structures, hotel, terminal and office space, and areas to house additional ticketing, check-in, baggage claim and rental car facilities. New amenities such as retail, banquet facilities and 215,000 square feet of office space were also part of the program.

The curtain wall exterior, which includes interior single-loaded corridors separated by an open-air space, draws light deeper into all realms of the building. Simplicity of the structure is maintained as passengers are drawn down a single path along the building's edge, allowing them to relish the organic landscape as they progress. Humanized, user-friendly attributes are addressed in all areas of the design. For example, special attention was given to clearly denoted and efficient circulation flows. The layout and design of the structure functionally and aesthetically unites the entire system.

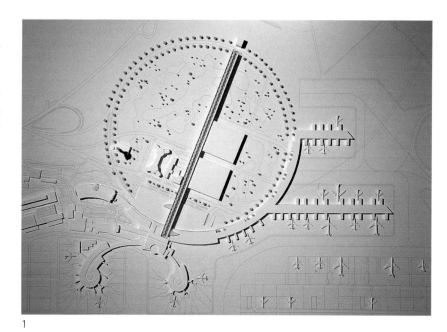

1

2

3

4

5

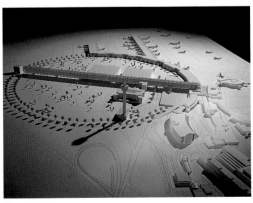

6

1 Site plan
2 Aerial view of model
3 Model detail
4 Airfield view of model
5 Landside view of model
6 Aerial view of model

1   Exterior model
Below:
     Massing model
3&4   Interior renderings

1

3

4

Central Terminal Redevelopment and Expansion at Seattle-Tacoma International Airport

Selected from a group of renowned architects, our firm was chosen to design the expansion and redevelopment of the 50-year-old Central Terminal at Seattle-Tacoma International Airport in June of 1998. The reiteration of our design philosophy in the November 1998 Port of Seattle draft vision statement for this project paved the way for a very cohesive and collaborative effort in the design and construction of the terminal. The draft vision statement read:

The excitement of travel that existed when this airport was built has waned for many of today's travelers. As many more people have taken to the skies and our numbers of passengers have increased, passenger facilities that our parents built have become tired and overworked. Now we have the opportunity to recreate the excitement of travel and at the same time provide the passenger comforts and conveniences to greater numbers of travelers and different types of passengers of this new age, such as children, families, holiday travelers, business hubbing travelers and others.

We also have the opportunity to make an expression with this architecture that we are about to create. ... It should be an expression of this place, Seattle-Tacoma, as a 'gateway'. The architecture should be expressive of this place, of the climate, landscape, the natural environment and the people [... the] air and quality of light, the views to and from. (Fentress Bradburn Architects, Central Terminal Redevelopment: Basis of Design – Schematic Design Phase II, Executive Summary, 1998, p. 2)

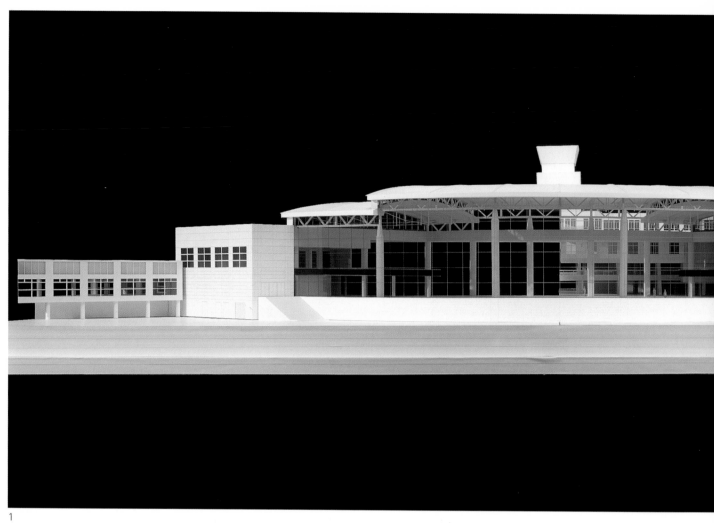

1

2

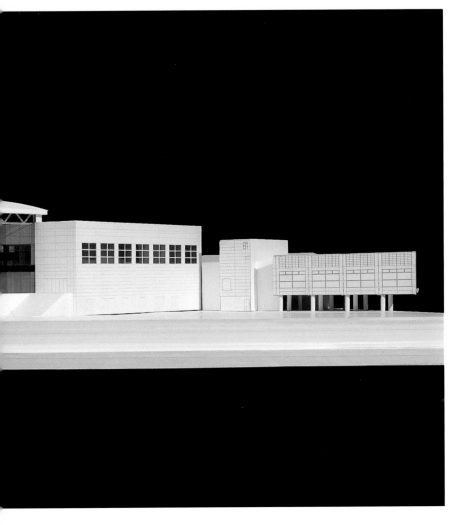

1 Exterior airside elevation
2 Grand central space

In keeping with our contextual regional design philosophy, we have created a design for a central civic space with distinctive commercial and concession opportunities, art exhibits and space for interactive educational experiences. The Central Terminal is the "jewel box" that ties the collage of redeveloped concourses and terminal renovations into a cohesive representation of Seattle and Tacoma's past, present and future.

The Central Terminal redevelopment project involves the creation of a grand central space that will become a recognizable orientation point at the center of the airport's main terminal. Our design provides passengers with a greater variety of retail, dining and entertainment opportunities than currently exists at the airport. This space will be located along the main passenger flow to the concourses. The design will also simplify passenger flow through the main terminal as travelers easily find their way from curbside to gates.

The circulation routes are reminiscent of Seattle's renowned outdoor markets. Direct natural light together with custom lamp post-like light fixtures and hanging plants create an esplanade that directs passenger flows. Yet, passengers feel nestled in an interior environment with distinct character and personality, conducive to relaxation

as well as retail and concession shopping. Overall, the airport will be able to provide an increased level of customer service and generate a reliable, substantial source of non-airline revenue.

The main exterior design feature is a large expanse of glass with views to the airfield and the region beyond. Connection with the local environment is established through a highly transparent frontal façade that allows the outdoors to flood into the interior—an architectural constant among the region's prominent facilities. While the state-of-the-art facility is prominent and innovative in its new design, architectural elements from the original 1947 Art Deco design are referenced in the security pavilions. For instance, the patterns embedded in the frit glass resemble the custom precast screen design of the old departure gates.

Also encompassed in the Central Terminal's expansion and redevelopment program is the need to provide seismic protection and stability to the oldest part of the existing airport. The seismic upgrade will provide an increased level of public safety as required by current State building codes. In addition, security checkpoints were relocated to concourses A/B and C/D, establishing post-security access to the new central terminal and existing concourses.

1

Reina Sofia Airport in Tenerife-Sur

Located in the Atlantic Ocean among the Canary Islands and just off the coast of Spain, Tenerife-Sur is a tourist hotspot for Europeans and acts as an economic engine for its Spanish authority. The island has two distinct climates: the northern section is green and lush, while the southern section is largely desert and volcanic rock. A large inactive volcano, situated centrally, defines the separation between north and south.

Fentress Bradburn Architects participated in an open international design competition for the Reina Sofia Airport in Tenerife-Sur. Located on the southwestern side of the island and imbedded on a hillside of volcanic rock, the site for the new airport complex is one of the most challenging aspects of this project, largely due to a grade change from one side of the apron to the other.

Our overall design concept was inspired by the sailing vessels that frequent the island. Covered in fabric, the variegated open-air, enclosed structure keeps travelers integrated with the tropical experience throughout their journey. Soft sail-like canopies welcome arriving passengers at curbside before they enter into the ticketing and check-in hall, where the gracefully arching roof trusses are supported by approximately 80-foot-tall curtain walls. Enlarged-scale curbside canopies also protect passengers waiting on the open-air train platform from inclement weather. Four three-dimensional trusses form a pyramid over the central pod of each satellite concourse, a remote concourse with a central pod and up to four radiating concourses.

1   Aerial view of central retail-pod model
2   Model of satellite concourse central retail-pod
3   Detail of curbside
4   Section model from curbside to ticketing hall
    to people-mover

2

3

4

The program called for an airport capable of processing over 1,200 people at any given time. Due to the current and anticipated quantity of passengers, space-planning efforts of the satellite concourse design were the key challenging elements in the design competition. Operating as the central focus of the facility, where passengers arrive and depart by means of an automated people mover (APM), satellites were designed to contain all of the airport's retail mall space.

Tropical elements were also incorporated into various aspects of interiors. Live palm trees bring the outdoors inside and provide a more tropical lounge for people as they either arrive or depart. Nestled among the palm trees, rest areas afford a relaxing interim for passengers with extended layovers. Floor patterns reminiscent of local foliage relate to the surrounding environment and aid circulation flow by directing passengers through the ticketing hall, or to connecting concourses. The light and airy feeling that is carried throughout the facility provides an excellent iconographic civic structure for the island.

APPENDIX A

1974
Dallas-Fort Worth International Airport opens

September 1978
Special Airport Task Force is appointed by the Denver Chamber of Commerce

November 1988
Mayor Federico Peña appoints the Blue Ribbon Advisory Committee

January 1989
New airport master plan completed

March 1989
Selection process for Passenger Terminal Architect begins

May 1989
Denver voters pass a new airport referendum

September 1989
Ground-breaking ceremony for Denver International Airport; site preparation and construction begin

April 1990
Final design awaits City and County of Denver's decision regarding location of Federal Inspections Area and terminal configuration

June 1990
Fentress Bradburn Architects propose design revisions to original concept including new roof design

July 1990
Fentress Bradburn Architects authorized to begin construction documents; Fentress Bradburn Architects reworks design efforts to reduce schedule by eight months

October 1990
Bid date for AGTS platform and stations

January 1991
American Airlines is scheduled to make another presentation regarding the BAE baggage system; the project management team has indicated that if the airlines want to construct such a system, the City would consider a proposal; PCL completes excavation for overall areas of the project; Weitz Cohen is given notice to proceed with excavation for train station platform and terminal

February 1991
Continental Airlines declares bankruptcy and this, combined with the Persian Gulf War, sheds doubt on the financial feasibility of the airport, according to the project management team

June 1991
Bid dates for terminal complex structure, finishes, parking structures and bridges

July 1991
United Airlines commits to establishing a hub operation at Denver International Airport

September 1991
Focus is directed to baggage and communication systems; major program revisions for United Airlines

October 1991
Bid date for Airport Office Building

December 1991
Preliminary notice to proceed given to BAE Automated Systems for baggage system

January 1992
Work behind schedule due to delivery problems, accidents, weather delays; City of Denver decides to extend the automated baggage system to the entire airport

APPENDIX A

TIMELINE

February 1992
Amendment to Fentress Bradburn Architects' contract to include tenant changes within the United Airlines terminal and expansion of the parking structure

February 1992
Bid date for Airport Office Building tenant improvements

March – July 1992
Passenger Terminal Building work on schedule

July 1992
Main concerns (baggage-handling system redesign, airline-requested changes and security system integration) are identified by the project management team; construction of the Teflon-coated fiberglass tensile-membrane roof structure begins

August 1992
A complete mezzanine level is ordered to be added to Level 3 to accommodate the needs of BAE Automated Systems; work to be accelerated to maintain schedule

August 1992
Bid date for additional parking structures

October 1992
Tenant changes, work stoppage due to impending changes, unsigned airline contracts and the slow process of selecting tenants and concessionaires remain major issues, causing significant obstacles; terminal progress slows due to construction of the additional mezzanine floor

November 1992
Teflon-coated fiberglass tensile-membrane roof structure is complete

January 1993
Federico Peña is appointed as U.S. Secretary of Transportation

March 1993
Opening date postponed to October 28, 1993,
by Denver Mayor Wellington Webb

October 1993
Opening date postponed to December 19, 1993,
by Denver Mayor Wellington Webb

December 1993
Opening date postponed to March 9, 1994, by
Denver Mayor Wellington Webb

January 1994
Denver International Airport ready to open except
for the baggage system

March 1994
Opening date postponed to May 15, 1994, by
Denver Mayor Wellington Webb

May 1994
Opening date postponed with no set date

July 1994
City of Denver installs $50 million conventional
baggage system

August 1994
Mayor Webb announces opening date to be
February 28, 1995

February 1995
Denver International Airport opens

APPENDIX B

MATERIALS AND DESIGN FEATURES

Area of Passenger Terminal Complex at Denver International Airport: *two million square feet*

Construction Cost of the Passenger Terminal Complex: *$455,000,000*

Structural Materials: *steel, precast concrete and Teflon-coated fiberglass*

Exterior Materials: *Teflon-coated fiberglass, precast architectural concrete, aluminum curtain wall, painted mullions and green glass with a low-e coating to enhance the energy efficiency; precast remains consistent between both the Passenger Terminal and the Airport Office Buildings*

Interior Materials: *granite, stainless steel, glass and carpet*

Roof Height: *126 feet from the lower level of the Great Hall floor to the highest peak*

Roof Weight: *400 tons (two pounds per square foot)*

Number of Gates: *124 ultimately operational as of 1999; the terminal frontage provided to park aircraft is 15,880 linear feet*

Runways: *12 ultimately operational, five built; the configuration provides three parallel north–south runways, two on the east side of the Passenger Terminal Complex, and two east–west runways, one north and one south of the complex; the three north–south runways are spaced to permit three simultaneous arrivals; Denver International Airport is the only airport in the world with this capability*

Approach Road: *Peña Boulevard, a four-lane highway, was constructed to provide access from Interstate 70 to Denver International Airport*

Electrical Lines: *Denver International Airport has a dual-source electrical service provided by two substations located north and south of the airport; the redundant service eliminates the need for emergency generators*

A P P E N D I X C

DESIGN AND CONSTRUCTION CREDITS

Fentress Bradburn Architects
Key Personnel

Curtis Fentress
Design Principal

James Bradburn
Managing Principal

Michael O. Winters
Design Director

Barbara Hochstetler Fentress
Director of Interior Design

Thom Walsh
Project Manager and Director of Airports

Brian Chaffee
Project Designer International Arrivals Building

Brit Probst
Project Administrator

John Kudrycki
Manager of Quality Assurance

Joseph Solomon
Technical Coordination

John Salisbury
Technical Coordination

Fred Pax
CADD Translations

Dave Thompkins
CADD Translations

Les Stuart
CADD Translations

Jayne Coburn
Office Administrator

Todd Britton
Model Crafter

Galen Bailey
Model Crafter

Amy Solomon
Model Crafter

Fentress Bradburn Architects and Designers

Rick Burkett

Garrett Christnacht

John Gagnon

Mike Gengler

Greg Gidez

Warren Hogue

Charles Johns

Anthia Kappos

Lauren Lee

Mike Miller

Garry Morris

Jack Mousseau

A. Chris Olson

Brian Ostler

Teri Paris

Bob Root

Tim Roush

Sam Tyner

Mark A. Wagner

Jun Xia

Contractors

PCL/Harbert

Hensel Phelps

MA Mortenson

Weitz/Cohen

Alvarado

AEG Westinghouse

BAE Automated Systems

Consultants

Western Industrial Contractors

S.A. Miro, Inc.

Martin/Martin

Severud Associates Consulting

HDR Engineering, Inc.

Architectural Energy Corporation

Black & Veatch

Abeyta Engineering Consultants

Rolf Jensen & Associates, Inc.

Rowan, Williams, Davies and Irwin

Tammy Kudrycki Design

Pouw & Associates

Carl Walker Engineers

David L. Adams Associates

Roos Szynskie, Incorporated

Riegel Associates

CTL/Thompson

Heitmann & Associates

Shen, Milsom & Wilke

Hesselberg Keesee & Associates

Aerospace Services International

Horst Berger

Bertram A. Bruton

APPENDIX D

Denver International Airport

George Doughty
Director of Aviation

William Smith
Director of Public Works

Ginger Evans
Associate Director of Aviation

Jim Dunlop
Assistant Director of Aviation/Operations

Bob Stroch
Chief of Construction

Hana Rocek
Manager of Design

Reginald Norman
Project Manager

Max Anthis
Project Manager of Ground Access

Greg McMenamin
Architect

David Dixon
CADD Manager

Emil Gadeken
*Manager for Data
& Communication Systems*

Barbara Payne
Intern

Project Management
Greiner Engineering/
Morrison-Knudsen Engineering

APPENDIX E

AIRPORT DESIGN AWARDS

As testament to Fentress Bradburn Architects' problem-solving and creative design approach, they have been honored by an extraordinary number of professional awards for design excellence on State, national and international levels. In 20 years of practice, Fentress Bradburn Architects have received 140 awards for design excellence, 47 of which are national and/or international awards, as well as 12 awards for excellence in design for transportation projects.

Denver International Airport Passenger Terminal Complex

Design for Transportation Honor Award, U.S. Department of Transportation, 1995

Grand Award, Gold Nugget Awards, Pacific Coast Builders Conference, 1995

Honor Award, American Institute of Architects, Colorado Chapter, 1994

Honor Award, American Institute of Architects, Western Mountain Region, 1994

Honor Award, American Institute of Architects, Denver Chapter, 1994

Excellence Award, Consulting Engineering Council of Colorado, 1993

Excellence Award, New York Association of Consulting Engineers, 1993

Inchon International Airport Passenger Terminal

International Design Competition   First Place Award, 1992

Doha International Airport Passenger Terminal Complex

International Design Competition   First Place Award, 1994

PHOTOGRAPHY CREDITS

National Air & Space Museum, Smithsonian Institute (S1neg#79-1992) 8
Port Authority of New York 9
Bruce Clarke 10 (top)
Buddy Jenssen 10 (bottom)
Gary Conner 11 (top)
Michael Brinson 11 (bottom)
Ed Bernstein 12, 58
Timothy Hursley cover, 13, 34, 85, 86, 88, 92, 93, 94, 96, 104, 112, 114, 116, 118
Roger Whitacre 14
Rocky Mountain News 20
Cyrus McCrimmon 21
Ron Johnson 23, 24 (right), 26, 28, 29, 30, 31, 36, 42, 50, 91, 98, 102, 106, 107, 110, 123 (top) 130, 131, 140, 146,150, 151, 152, 154, 156, 157
JL Curtis Photography 18, 22, 24 (left), 46 (bottom)
Bob Perzel 25, 62 (left), 63, 64 (top), 65 (top), 66, 67, 68 (top), 69, 72 (top), 73, 77
Nick Merrick-Hedrich Blessing 52, 84, 90, 97, 108, 109, 113
Alex Sweetman 54, 55, 56, 57, 60 (bottom), 62 (right), 64 (bottom), 65
George Kochaniec Jr. 59
Dave Buresh 60 (top)
Brian Brainerd 68
Glen Martin 72 (bottom)
Jay Koelzer 74
Joe Poellot 78, 79
Glynn Asakawa 80 (bottom)
Ellen Jaskol & United Airlines 84 (top)
James W. Jenson 100
KACA (Korean Airport Construction Authority) 122, 123, 124, 125
Studio Qatar 135, 139
Jack Mousseau 153 (top)
Curtis Fentress 15, 17

ASSOCIATE ARCHITECTS

Inchon International Airport
Korean Architects Collaborative International
Munich International Airport
Fentress Bradburn Moore
Vienna International Airport
Fentress Bradburn Moore
New Terminal at Madrid-Barajas International Airport
Oriol Arquitectura, S.L.